Dime's Worth of Difference

Beyond the Lesser of Two Evils

Dime's Worth of Difference
Beyond the Lesser of Two Evils

Edited by
Alexander Cockburn
and Jeffrey St. Clair

CounterPunch
PETROLIA

AK
PRESS

First published by
CounterPunch and AK Press 2004
© CounterPunch 2004
All rights reserved

CounterPunch *PO Box 228 Petrolia, California, 95558*

AK Press *674A 23rd St, Oakland, California 94612-1163*
www.akpress.org

PO Box 12766, Edinburgh, Scotland EH89YE
www.akuk.org

ISBN 1-904859-03-8

Library of Congress Cataloguing in-Publication data
Dime's Worth of Difference: 2004105036

A catalog record for this book is available from the Library of Congress

Typeset in Tyfa and Stainless.
Printed and bound in Canada.

Designed by Tiffany Wardle
Cover Illustration by Michael Dickinson

Contents

ALL VOTING IS A SORT of gaming, like checkers or backgammon, with a slight moral tinge to it, a playing with right and wrong, with moral questions; and betting naturally accompanies it. The character of the voters is not staked. I cast my vote, perchance, as I think right; but I am not vitally concerned that that right should prevail. I am willing to leave it to the majority. Its obligation, therefore, never exceeds that of expediency. Even voting for the right is doing nothing for it. It is only expressing to men feebly your desire that it should prevail. A wise man will not leave the right to the mercy of chance, nor wish it to prevail through the power of the majority. There is but little virtue in the action of masses of men. When the majority shall at length vote for the abolition of slavery, it will be because they are indifferent to slavery, or because there is but little slavery left to be abolished by their vote. They will then be the only slaves. Only his vote can hasten the abolition of slavery who asserts his own freedom by his vote.

Henry David Thoreau, On Civil Disobedience

IT IS ONE THING TO trample a kid half to death or to death, that is bad enough; but it is quite another thing to then be told by the agents of that oppression, 'be patient, we will do better tomorrow.' The question will cross your mind just for a moment: 'You will do what better tomorrow?' No, no, the militancy and the vitality that I heard in the music here today comes from the kind of energy which allows you, which in fact forces you to examine everything, taking nothing for granted. To say that it has been this way for the last two hundred years but that it will not be this way for the next five minutes. That if, for example, you don't think you can work in the Democratic Party, you don't have to. There are other things. It is a vitality in short which allows you to believe, to act on the belief that it is your country and your responsibility to your country is to free it, and to free it you have to change it.

James Baldwin speech to the Student Nonviolent
Coordinating Committee (SNCC) Conference on Food
and Freedom, Washington D.C. November 1963

THERE AIN'T A DIME'S WORTH of difference between 'em, hoss.

Waylon Jennings

Chapter 1

"The central political issue in this first decade
of the twenty-first century is the decay of the
American political system and of the two
prime parties that share the spoils. Wherever
one looks, at the gerrymandered districts, the
balloting methods, the fundraising, corruption
fumes like vapors from a vast swamp."

Alexander Cockburn
**Presidential Elections:
Not as Big a Deal as They Say**

Alexander Cockburn

Presidential Elections:
Not as Big a Deal as They Say

RESHETS OF CREATIVITY AND EXCITEMENT PULSING INTO the nation's bloodstream, improvements in the general quality of life, have nothing to do with the presidential elections rolling around every four years, which rouse expectations far in excess of what they actually deserve. As registers of liberal or conservative political potency, American presidential elections seldom coincide with shifts in the tempo of political energy across the country. As vehicles for the ventilation of popular concerns, they are hopelessly inadequate, and should be severely downgraded on the entertainment calendars.

Take a couple of profound changes in the quality of life over the past thirty years. You can now buy good coffee, shoulder to shoulder at the coffee stand with a construction worker with hair in a ponytail and a tactful gold ring in his ear, anywhere in America from Baltimore to San Pedro, Key West to Michigan's Upper Peninsula. No American political party ever wrote a commitment to better cappuccino into its platform. From the late 60s on, the hippies, despising the dank turreens of perma-perked Robusta coffee, roasted Arabica coffee beans. Small roasters held up the banner of quality. Then, when Communism foundered (a collapse that owed nothing to Ronald Reagan) and Uncle Sam no longer had any incentive to fix the coffee markets and prices benefiting its prime Latin American cold war allies, growers from New Guinea, Costa Rica, Kenya and elsewhere where able to send better Arabica beans to our shores. The quality of life went up markedly. Of course, at the level of national US "policy", the World Bank, dominated by the US, then threw billions at Vietnam a few years ago to grow very bad coffee, which undercut these same quality producers.

The bread's got better too and so have the vegetables, thanks once again to the hippies, organic farms, farmers' markets and community-supported agricultural networks. No thanks here to party platforms, or presidential candidates, or Congress people, all of whom are in the pay of the big food companies, which have killed more Americans than the Pentagon by a factor of hundreds, and which, having failed to outlaw genuinely organic food, have now captured its name and altered its meaning. Over the past thirty years the meat's got worse, as small wholesale butchers have gone to the wall, bankrupted by the coalition of food regulators and big food processors, the latter industry now dominated by two vast meatpacking combines, Tyson and Smithfield.

You want to see fascism in action in America? Look beyond the Patriot Act, engendered in the Clinton era with the Counter-Terrorism and Effective Death Penalty Act of 1996, and consummated by bipartisan agreement after 9/11, 2001. Try your local health department, bearing down on some small business. Better still, visit family court. No candidate goes out on the hustings and pledges to reform family courts so that their actions have some detectable linkage to the US Constitution and the Bill of Rights. No Republican or Democratic platform committee has ever devoted a paragraph to family courts. Yet there, day after day, week after week, relationships are destroyed, children severed irrevocably from parents and extended kin, fathers forbidden access to their children, their wages garnished, their bank accounts looted, staggering fines levied, without the possibility of challenge. (And no, this is not the defeated whine of a wronged dad.)

Judicial appointments are often the last frantic argument of a liberal urging all back in under the Big Democratic Tent. But these days the decay of liberalism is reflected in the quality of judges installed in the federal district courts. The Blacks, Douglases, Marshalls and Brennans were conjured to greatness by historical circumstance first, and only later by the good fortune of confirmed nomination. Today's historical circumstances are not throwing up Blacks, Douglases, Marshalls and Brennans, even if a Democratic president has the opportunity and backbone to nominate them. And at the level of the US Supreme Court, history is captious. The two best of the current bunch, John Paul Stevens and David Souter, were nominated by Republican presidents, Gerald Ford and G.W.H. Bush. You'll as likely find a maverick on the conservative as on the liberal end of a judicial bench.

Every four years liberals unhitch the cart and put it in front of the horse, arguing that the only way to a safer, better tomorrow will be if everyone votes for the Democratic nominee. But unless the nominee and Congress are shoved forward by social currents too strong for them to defy or ignore, then nothing except the usual bad things will transpire. In the American Empire of today, the default path chosen by the country's supreme commanders and their respective parties is never toward the good. Our task is not to dither in distraction over the lesser of two evil prospects, which turns out to be only a detour along the same highway.

The way they are now set up, presidential contests focused well nigh exclusively on the candidates of the two major parties are worse than useless in furnishing an opportunity for any useful national debate. In 2000 Ralph Nader got about five minutes face time on the national networks. It would be an improvement, and certainly more interesting, if the big four-year debate centered on which definitions of mental complaints should be added to or subtracted from the *American Psychiatric Association's Diagnostic and Statistical Manual of Mental Disorders* which governs official diagnoses of America's mental and emotional condition and which is revised every few years. Recalling one such revision in the 1970s, Phil Johnson, a gay man from Dallas, said in the film *After Stonewall*, "I went to bed one night,

I was sick and depraved, and when I woke up the next morning I discovered I'd been cured". In 2004 Bush could have campaigned for the removal of ADD, arguing it's a natural and useful condition, emblem of presidential greatness, and pledging to end this national affliction.

The central political issue in this first decade of the 21st century is the decay of the American political system and of the two prime parties that share the spoils. Wherever one looks, at the gerrymandered districts, the balloting methods, the fundraising, corruption fumes like vapors from a vast swamp. In the House of Representatives today, only some 35 seats are in serious contention. The rest have been gerrymandered into permanent incumbencies. Congress itself is an infinitely drearier, more conformist place than it was two or three decades ago. Vivid souls like Wright Patman and Henry Gonzalez of Texas, in whose hearts the coals of populist insurgency still glowed, are long gone. Today, where are the Ernest Gruenings, the Wayne Morses, the Harold Hughes, who stood out against the rush to war in the Vietnam years? In the US Senate, amid the march on Iraq we heard an eloquent echo from Robert Byrd, and from one or two others including Ted Kennedy. In the House, entirely alone on one occasion, Barbara Lee. In the House you can count the true mavericks on the fingers of both hands, and almost always you'll find there Ron Paul, the libertarian Republican from Texas' second district, running south along the Gulf coast toward Corpus Christi, whence Ronald Reagan once quavered theatrically, to a respectful press, that the Sandinista army would come blazing up State Highway 77 from Harlingen, after a march Hannibal would have envied, from Nicaragua, through Honduras, Guatemala and Mexico.

On the calendar of standard-issue American politics, the quadrennial presidential contests have offered, across the past 40 years, a relentlessly shrinking menu. To go back to 1964, the Democratic convention that nominated Lyndon Johnson saw the Democratic Party powers scorn the legitimate claim of Fannie Lou Hamer and her fellow crusaders in the Mississippi Freedom Democratic Party to be the lawful Mississippi delegation. The black insurgents went down to defeat in a battle that remained etched in the political consciousness of those who partook in or even observed the fray. There was political division, the bugle blare and saber slashes of genuine struggle.

By 1968 there was still a run against LBJ, albeit more polite in form, with Eugene McCarthy's challenge to Lyndon Johnson. McCarthy's call for schism was an eminently respectable one, from a man who had risen through the US Senate as an orthodox Democratic cold-war liberal. He himself saw the limits of his "test of the system". "It might have been better", he remarked to the reporter Andrew Kopkind in the midst of his campaign, "to let things run wild – to have a peasants' revolt. Maybe it would have been better to stand back and let people light fires on the hill." As he well knew, the Democratic Party exists to suppress peasants' revolts and douse fires on the hill.

Four years later, when George McGovern again kindled the antiwar torch, the party's established powers, the labor chieftains and the money men, did their best to douse his modest smoulder, deliberately surrendering the field to Richard Nixon, for whom many of them voted. And yet, by today's standards, that strange man Nixon, under whose aegis the Environmental Protection Agency was founded, the Occupational Safety and Health Act passed, Earth Day first celebrated, and Keynesianism accepted as a fact of life, would have been regarded as impossibly radical. And he did these things because of the historical circumstances which forced him in that direction.

With Jimmy Carter came the omens of neoliberalism, which later flowered in the Clinton years under the logo of the Democratic Leadership Council. Resistance came in 1976 with Barry Commoner and his Citizens' Party, then in 1979-80 with Senator Ted Kennedy's challenge to Carter for the nomination under the battle standard of old-line New Deal liberalism. There was also Republican John Anderson's independent run as a moderate.

The two Democratic presidential nominees of the 1980s, Fritz Mondale in 1984 and Michael Dukakis in 1988, saw party leaders and pundits massed protectively, standing shoulder to shoulder against the last coherent left populist campaign in America mounted within the framework of the Democratic Party, by Jesse Jackson and the Rainbow Coalition. The Democratic Party gave its rebuttal to Jackson and the Rainbow with Clinton in 1992 and again in 1996. As JoAnn Wypijewski succinctly puts it, "By a brisk accounting of 1993 to 2000, the black stripe of the Rainbow got the Crime Bill, women got 'welfare reform', labor got NAFTA, gays and lesbians got the Defense of Marriage Act. Even with a Democratic Congress in the early years, the peace crowd got no cuts in the military; unions got no help on the right to organize; advocates of DC statehood got nothing (though statehood would virtually guarantee two more Democratic Senate seats and more representation in the House); the single-payer crowd got worse than nothing. Between Clinton's inaugural and the day he left office, 700,000 more persons were incarcerated, mostly minorities; today one in eight black men is barred from voting because of prison, probation or parole."

It was just before his re-election campaign, in 1996, that Bill Clinton took for his own the Republican proposal for "welfare reform", even worse than his original proposal for "reform" in 1992. Victory was assured, but he followed through anyway on a bill he knew was rotten. Liberals were aghast but did nothing. There was no insurgency, no rocking of the boat, no "divisive" challenge on that or anything else. The Democratic Party, from DLC governors to liberal public-interest groups mustered around their leader and marched into the late Nineties arm in arm along the path sign-posted toward the greatest orgy of corporate theft in the history of the planet, deregulation of banking and food safety, rates of logging six times those achieved in the subsequent Bush years, a war on Yugoslavia, a vast expansion of the death penalty, re-affirmation of racist drug laws, the foundations of the Patriot Act.

Through the Clinton years the Democratic Party remained "united" in fealty to corporate corruption and right-wing class viciousness, and so inevitably and appropriately, the Nader-centered independent challenge was born, modestly in 1996, strongly in 2000 and again in 2004, joining such other independent campaigns as Ross Perot's, whose entrance on the scene in 1992 actually cost G.H.W. Bush re-election but never provoked such hysteria on the Republican end of the spectrum as burst over Nader's head in 2000 and again, even more hysterically in 2004. The rationale for Nader's challenge was as sound as it was for Henry Wallace half a century earlier. I quote from *The Third Party*, a little pamphlet by Adam Lapin published in 1948 in support of Wallace and his Progressive Party, found in a box of left literature sent to me in June 2004 by my friend Honey Williams of Carmel Highlands, cleaning house after the death of her uncle Dick Criley. (She'd promised me some crab apple scions for grafting, and I was a mite put out to find souvenirs of Dick's political library, such as Plekhanov and Lenin, lurking in the box instead.)

"Every scheme of the lobbyists to fleece the public became law in the 80th Congress. And every constructive proposal to benefit the common people gathered dust in committee pigeonholes…. The bipartisan bloc, the Republocratic cabal which ruled Congress and made a mockery of President Roosevelt's economic bill of rights, also wrecked the Roosevelt foreign policy…. A new foreign policy was developed. This policy was still gilded with the good words of democracy. But its Holy Grail was oil….

"The Democratic administration carries the ball for Wall Street's foreign policy. And the Republican party carries the ball for Wall Street's domestic policy.... Of course the roles are some-times interchangeable. It was President Truman who broke the 1946 railroad strike, asked for legislation to conscript strikers and initiated the heavy fines against the miners' union.

"On occasion President Truman still likes to lay an occasion-al verbal wreath on the grave of the New Deal.... But the hard facts of roll call votes show that Democrats are voting more and more like Republicans. If the Republican Taft-Hartley bill became law over the President's veto, it was because many of the Democrats allied themselves to the Republicans. Only 71 House Democrats voted to sustain the Prersident's veto while 106 voted to override it. In the Senate 20 Democrats voted to override the veto and 22 voted to sustain it."

There you have it: the law that was to enable capital to destroy organized labor when it became convenient was passed by a bipartisan vote (and with more than just southern Democ-rats), something you will never learn from the AFL-CIO, or from a thousand hoarse throats at Democratic rallies when the candi-date is whoring for the labor vote. In the Clinton years, union membership as a percentage of the work force dropped, as well it might, because he did nothing to try to change laws or to intervene in disputes.

Clinton presided over passage of NAFTA, insulting labor further with the farce of side agreements on labor rights that would never be enforced. End result: half the companies involved in organizing drives in the US intimidate workers by saying that a union vote will force the company to leave town; 30 percent of them fire the union activists (about 20,000 workers a year); only one in seven organizing drives has a chance of going to a vote, and of those that do result in a yes vote for the union, less than one in five has any success in getting a contract.

So while many saw the rapid decline in union membership as just a melancholy index of the passing of the old economy, making way for a cornucopia of New Economy jobs that would be high-paying affairs with plenty of stock options for workers, the reality is otherwise. Most New Economy jobs are in fact low-tech, low-skill, low-paying jobs with no future. Polls suggest that 60 percent of non-unionized workers say they would join a union if they had a chance. The Democrats have produced no laws, indeed have campaigned against laws that would make that attainable. John Kerry's proposal on the minimum wage in 2004 would raise it to $7 an hour by 2007, which would bring a full-time worker up to two-thirds of the poverty level.

One useful way of estimating how little separates the Democratic and Republican parties, and particularly their presidential nominees, is to tot up the issues on which there is tacit agreement either as a matter of principle or with an expedient nod-and-wink that these are not matters suitable to be discussed in any public forum, beyond *pro forma* sloganeering: the role of the Federal Reserve, trade policy, economic redistribution, the role and budget of the CIA and other intelligence agencies, nuclear disarmament, allocation of military procurement, reduction of the military budget, the roles and policies of the World Bank, International Monetary Fund and kindred multilateral agencies, crime, punishment and the prison explosion, the war on drugs, corporate welfare, energy policy, forest policy, the destruction of small farmers and ranchers, Israel, the corruption of the political system.

Let us suppose that a Democratic candidate arrives in the White House, at least rhetorically committed to reform, as happened with Jimmy Carter in 1977 and Clinton in 1993. Both had Democratic majorities in Congress. Battered from their first weeks for any unorthodox nominees and for any deviation from Wall Street's agenda in their first budgets, both had effectively lost any innovative purchase on the system by the end of their first six months, and there was no pressure from the left to hold them to their pledges. Carter was torn apart by the press for his

Office of Management Budget director nominee, Bert Lance; Clinton, for gays in the military.

As a candidate in 1984 Mondale advanced the schedule of surrender to the period of his doomed candidacy, filing to change his political identity to that of Ronald Reagan by September of that campaign year. Reagan claimed that Nicaragua was exporting revolution to the rest of Latin America and so did Mondale. Reagan said Nicaragua should be "pressured" till it mended its ways, and so did Mondale. Reagan said he would invade Nicaragua if it bought 28-year-old Soviet MIG-21s and so did Mondale. Reagan blamed the missile crisis in Europe on the Russians and so did Mondale. Reagan wanted to hike the military budget and so did Mondale. Reagan was bad on the Middle East, and Mondale was worse. Mondale promised to raise taxes and cut social spending. Four years later, battered by charges he was a closet liberal, Dukakis swiftly collapsed.

By the end of April 1993, Clinton had sold out the Haitian refugees; handed Africa policy to a Bush appointee, Herman Cohen, thus giving Jonas Savimbi the green light in Angola to butcher thousands; put Israel's lobbyists in charge of Mideast policy; bolstered the arms industry with a budget in which projected spending for 1993-94 was higher in constant dollars than average spending in the Cold War from 1950 onward; increased secret intelligence spending; maintained full DEA funding; put Wall Street in charge of national economic strategy; sold out on grazing and mineral rights on public lands; pushed NAFTA forward; plunged into the "managed care" disaster offered by him and Hillary Rodham Clinton as "health reform".

By the end of May 1993, as any kind of progressive challenge to business-as-usual, the Clinton presidency had failed, even by the measure of its own timid promises. The recruitment of the old Nixon/Reagan/Bush hand David Gergen as the president's new public relations man signaled the surrender.

By 2000, with the Nader challenge, the most common reaction of Democrats was not debate but affront at the scandalous impertinence of his candidacy. A common reaction, both in 2000 with Gore and 2004 with Kerry, was the furious cry, "Don't talk to me about Gore!" or "I don't want to hear a word against Kerry!" It was as though the Democratic candidate was entombed, pending resurrection as president, with an honor guard of the National Organization of Women, the AFL-CIO, the League of Conservation Voters, Taxpayers for Justice, the NAACP. To open the tomb prematurely to admit the oxygen of life and criticism was to commit an intolerable blasphemy against political propriety. Amid the defilements of our political system, and the collapse of all serious political debate among the liberals and most of the left, the Democratic candidate becomes a kind of Hegelian Anybody, as in Anybody But...

The Kerry candidacy in 2004? As an inspirational candidate, even one whom polls predicted in early summer of 2004 would most likely end up in the White House, he was a dud, as damp a political squib as Michael Dukakis. Three terms in the US Senate have left almost no footprints of interest, except to Karl Rove's propagandists eager to transform this utterly conventional figure into a seditious radical, hell-bent on putting the Pentagon out of business. A seasoned staffer on one of the military appropriations committees described Kerry deprecatingly to me as "the ghost senator; around here he doesn't count for anything."

In the early days of his Senate career Kerry made headlines with hearings on contra-CIA drug smuggling and on BCCI , the crooked Pakistani bank linked to the CIA. Some of the Senate elders must have told him to mind his manners. The watchdog's barks died abruptly.

Kerry offers himself up mainly as a more competent manager of the Bush agenda, a steadier hand on the helm of the Empire. His pedigree is immaculate. He was a founding member of the Democratic Leadership Council, the claque of neoliberals that has sought to reshape it as a hawkish and pro-business party with a soft spot for abortion—essentially a stingier version of the Rockefeller Republicans. Kerry enthusiastically backed both of Bush's wars, and in June of 2004, at the very moment Bush signaled a desire to retreat, the senator called for 25,000 new troops to be sent to Iraq, with a plan for the US military to remain entrenched there for at least the next four years.

Kerry supported the Patriot Act without reservation or even much contemplation. Lest you conclude that this was a momentary aberration sparked by the post-9/11 hysteria, consider the fact that Kerry also voted for the two Clinton-era predecessors to the Patriot Act, the 1994 Crime Bill and the 1996 Counter-Terrorism and Effective Death Penalty Act.

Although, once his nomination was assured he regularly hammed it up in photo-ops with the barons of big labor, Kerry voted for NAFTA, the WTO and virtually every other job-slashing trade pact that came before the Senate. He courted and won the endorsement of nearly every police association in the nation, regularly calling for another 100,000 cops on the streets and even tougher criminal sanctions against victimless crimes. He refused to reconsider his fervid support for the insane war on drug users, which has destroyed families and clogged our prisons with more than 2 million people, many of them young black men, whom the draconian drug laws specifically target without mercy. Kerry backed the racist death penalty and minimum mandatory sentences.

Like Joe Lieberman, Kerry marketed himself as a cultural prude, regularly chiding teens about the kind of clothes they wear, the music they listen to and the movies they watch. But even Lieberman didn't go so far as to support the Communications Decency Act. Kerry did. Fortunately, even this Supreme Court had the sense to strike the law down, ruling that it trampled across the First Amendment.

All of this is standard fare for contemporary Democrats. But Kerry always went the extra mile. The senator cast a crucial vote for Clinton's bill to dismantle welfare for poor mothers and their children.

Bush's path to war was cleared by the Democrats, who were passive at best and deeply complicit at worst. House leader Dick Gephardt and Senator Joe Lieberman rushed to the White House to stand beside Bush in a Rose Garden war rally, where they pledged their support for the invasion of Iraq. Like John Kerry, vice-presidential pick John Edwards went along with the war. So did the rest of the Democratic leadership.

Most didn't even express regrets. Take Senate Majority leader Tom Daschle. Nearly a year after the war was launched, after every pretext had dissolved and the US military found itself mired in a bloody and hopeless occupation, Daschle pronounced himself satisfied with the war's progress.

Bush's performance and personality have been etched well past caricature by dozens of furious assailants, culminating in Michael Moore's *Fahrenheit 9/11*, the Democrats' prime campaign offering, and something the Republicans had coming to them for trying to nail Clinton for his affair with Monica Lewinsky. There is no need to labor the details of Bush's ghastly incumbency in these pages. He came by his fortune and his presidency dishonestly. Official rebirth in Christ did not lead him, a former sinner, to compassion but to vindictiveness. Genes and education turned into a Mendelian stew of all that's worst and most vulgar in the character traits of the elites of the Northeast and of Texas. A more limited occupant of the Oval Office is hard to recall or conceive of.

All the more striking therefore was it, as 2004 lurched forward, to mark the lack of exuberance, the poverty of expectations among Kerry's supporters. A more limited challenge to the incumbent was similarly hard to conceive of as, month by month, Kerry methodically disappointed one more liberal constituency. In April it was labor, admonished that Kerry's prime task would be to battle the deficit. In May and again in July it was women, informed that the candidate shared with the anti-abortion lobby its view of the relationship between conception and the start of life and that he would be prepared to nominate anti-choice judges. In June it was the anti-war legions, to whom Kerry pledged four more years of occupation in Iraq.

Thirty-eight years ago Martin Luther King was booed at a mass meeting in Chicago. Later, as he lay sleepless, he understood why:

"For twelve years I, and others like me, had held out radiant promises of progress. I had preached to them about my dream. I had lectured to them about the not too distant day when they would have freedom, 'all, here and now.' I urged them to have faith in America and in white society. Their hopes had soared. They were now booing because they felt we were unable to deliver on our promises. They were booing because we had urged them to have faith in people who had too often proved to be unfaithful. They were now hostile because they were watching the dream they had so readily accepted turn into a nightmare."

King, as Andrew Kopkind wrote at the time, quoting that passage, had been outstripped by his times and knew it. Nearly forty years later the times, and America's needs, have far, far outstripped the party which at that moment of despair in Chicago King saw as the betrayer of so many hopes. The creative task beckons to us, but on the battlefields of our choosing, not in the designated "protest space" sanctioned and invigilated by the powers that be.

Chapter 2

"'The general requirement of product differentiation in an electoral market', writes the economist Robert Pollin in his important book *Contours of Descent*, 'entails that at the margin any Democratic President will offer more social concessions than a Republican of the same cohort. But we should be careful not to make too much of such differences in the public stance of these two figures, as against the outcomes that prevail during their terms in office.'"

Alexander Cockburn
What Happened to the Economy Under Clinton?

ALEXANDER COCKBURN

What Happened to the Economy Under Clinton?

ENTER THE WORLD OF PAUL KRUGMAN, A WORLD EITHER dark (the eras of Bush One and Bush Two), or bathed in light (when Bill was king). Near the beginning of his collection of columns, *The Great Unraveling*, Krugman looks back on Clintontime. A throb enters his voice.

> At the beginning of the new millennium, then, it seemed that the United States was blessed with mature, skillful economic leaders, who in a pinch would do what had to be done. They would insist on responsible fiscal policies; they would act quickly and effectively to prevent a repeat of the jobless recovery of the early 90s, let alone a slide into Japanese-style stagnation. Even those of us who considered ourselves pessimists were basically optimists: we thought that bullish investors might face a rude awakening, but that it would all have a happy ending.... What happened to the good years?

A couple of hundred pages later:

> How did we get here? How did the American political system, which produced such reasonable economic leadership during the 1990s, lead us into our current morass of dishonesty and irresponsibility?

In the era of Bush Two Krugman became the Democrats' Clark Kent. A couple of times each week he burst onto the *New York Times* op-ed page in his blue jumpsuit, shouldering aside the Geneva Conventions and whacking the bad guys. For an economist he writes pretty good basic English. He lays about him with simple words like "liar", as applied to the Bush crowd, from the president on down. He makes liberals feel good, the way William Safire returned right-wingers their sense of self-esteem after Watergate.

Krugman shares, with no serious demur, all the central assumptions of the neo-liberal creed that has governed the prime institutions of the world capitalist system for the past generation and driven much of the world deeper, ever deeper into extreme distress.

Faintly, though not frequently, a riffle of doubt perturbed Krugman's paeans to the Clinton Age. "In an era of ever rising stock prices hardly any one noticed, but in the clear light of the morning after we can see that by the turn of the millennium something was very rotten in the state of American capitalism." It turns out he means only book-cooking of the Enron type, an outfit on whose advisory board Krugman once sat with an annual stipend of $50,000 and which he hailed in *Fortune* magazine in 1999 as the prime emblem of neoliberal corporate strategy.

"What we have", Krugman gurgled ecstatically in *Fortune* as he described the Enron trading room, "in a growing number of markets – phones, gas, electricity today – is a combination of deregulation that lets new companies enter and 'common carrier' regulation that prevents middlemen playing favorites, making freewheeling markets possible." Dr Pangloss couldn't have put it better.

You want to hear how Krugman's hymns to Enron worked out in practice? Listen to the tapes acquired by CBS News of to and fro between traders in Enron's West Coast trading room, as they contrived California's power crisis.

> "He just fucks California," says one Enron employee. "He steals money from California to the tune of about a million."
>
> "Will you rephrase that?" asks a second employee.
>
> "OK, he, um, he arbitrages the California market to the tune of a million bucks or two a day," replies the first.
>
> "If you took down the steamer, how long would it take to get it back up?" an Enron worker is heard saying.

"Oh, it's not something you want to just be turning on and off every hour. Let's put it that way," another says.

"Well, why don't you just go ahead and shut her down."

"They're fucking taking all the money back from you guys?" complains an Enron employee on the tapes. "All the money you guys stole from those poor grandmothers in California?"

"Yeah, grandma Millie, man."

"Yeah, now she wants her fucking money back for all the power you've charged right up, jammed right up her asshole for fucking $250 a megawatt hour."

In the concluding pages of a 426-page book where Krugman might have disturbed himself and his audience with difficult questions about the widening gap, right through Clinton time, between rich and poor across the world and here in the US, about the reasons why Clinton's bubble economy collapsed so abruptly, Krugman prefers to indulge himself in playing to the gallery, Thomas Friedman-style, with some Nader-bashing. He reprints a column written in July 2000, when Nader had decided that a third party candidacy was the only way he could forcefully raise just those "difficult and disturbing" questions the respectable and conventional Krugman shirks: "And was I the only person who shuddered when Mr. Nader declared that if he were president, he wouldn't reappoint Alan Greenspan – he would 'reeducate' him?"

Now suppose someone like Ralph Nader had re-educated Alan Greenspan prior to 1996, when the Fed chairman refused to impose the margin requirements on stock market speculators that would have punctured the bubble. It would have been a useful piece of schooling. But reeducation classes weren't on the agenda then any more than they are now, at least in Krugman's pages, so deferential to his heroes, like Robert Rubin, (Krugman reverently invokes "Rubinomics") who kicked aside regulatory impedimenta like Glass-Steagall and then sprinted out of his

Treasury job to cash in on the fruits of his deregulatory labors as co-director of the Citigroup conglomerate.

Krugman is a press agent, a busker, for Clintonomics. For him as for so many others on the liberal side, the world only went bad in January 2001. If a Democrat, pretty much any Democrat conventional enough to win Wall Street's approval, takes over again, maybe in 2005, the world will get better again.

Here's a signpost, pointing to what sort of choices or non-choices are really available to Americans in any election year. I found it planted in a dispatch from Ohio by Julian Borger in the London *Guardian* on November 3, 2003. By way of heralding an impending visit by Bush to Britain, Borger was edifying his readers with an account of Bush's America, in the form of a visit to a soup kitchen in Ohio where he reported that "hunger is an epidemic".

Since Ohio went for Bush in 2000 the state had lost one in six of its manufacturing jobs, many of them on account of the trade policies espoused by Clinton and now Bush. Two million of Ohio's 11 million population resorted to food charities in 2002, up 18 percent from 2001. In 25 major cities across the country in 2002 the need for emergency food rose an average of 19 percent.

In 2002 also another 1.7 million Americans slid below the poverty line, bringing the overall total to 34.6 million, one in eight as a proportion of the population. Over 13 million were children. The U.S. has the worst child poverty and the lowest life expectancy of all the world's industrialized countries.

About 31 million Americans are reckoned to be "food insecure", meaning they don't know where the next meal is coming from. Nine million are classed by the USDA as suffering "real hunger", defined bureaucratically as "an uneasy or painful sensation caused by lack of food due to lack of resources to obtain food".

THIS BRINGS US BACK TO CLINTON AND THE CLINTON YEARS. "The general requirement of product differentiation in an electoral market," the economist Robert Pollin writes in his important book *Contours of Descent: U.S. Economic Fractures and the Landscape of Global Austerity* (Verso), "entails that at the margin any Democratic president will offer more social concessions than a Republican of the same cohort. But we should be careful not to make too much of such differences in the public stance of these two figures, as against the outcomes that prevail during their terms in office."

For the truth of these observations, witness the aftermath of Clinton's welfare reforms and of bipartisan trade policies in Ohio.

Neoliberalism, a prime target of Pollin's timely book, is giving us an entire planet of tramps and millionaires, which the populist Ignatius Donnelly stigmatized as the economic emblems of the Gilded Age. When there are food riots in Buenos Aires, when bankrupted cotton farmers in Andrha Pradesh, south central India, swallow the pesticides whose "free market" price drove them into bankruptcy, the directors of the world political economy, bunkered down in Washington, should bear responsibility as much as for the hungry in Ohio.

Through the Clinton era, as through those of Reagan and both Bushes, the bargaining power of capital to cow workers, to make them toil harder for less real money, has increased inexorably.

When the bubble tide ebbed at the end of eight years of the Democrat Clinton, what did workers have by way of a permanent legacy? Clinton, Pollin bleakly concludes, "accomplished almost nothing in the way of labor laws or the broader policy environment to improve the bargaining situation for workers.... Moreover, conditions under Clinton worsened among those officially counted as poor."

In the overall economy the reserve army of the unemployed is swelling, just as reservists are increasingly manning US forces, as against the permanently employed forces of former times. The part-time soldiers recruited under neoliberalism's colors are being deployed against the fourth-generation warriors in the Third World that neoliberalism has played a huge share in creating.

On the domestic front Louis Uchitelle of the *New York Times* cited in late 2003 a Bureau of Labor Statistics survey of 10,000 people tracked since 1979 when "most were teenagers and the permanent layoff was just becoming a national phenomenon. They are in their 30s and 40s now, and over the years each has held, on average, 9.6 jobs."

The Clinton years did nothing to alter the rules of the neoliberal game that began in the Reagan/Thatcher era with the push to boost after-tax corporate profits, shift bargaining power to business, erode social protections for workers, make the rich richer, the middle tier at best stand still and the poor get poorer.

Across his 238 pages Pollin is unambiguous. "It was under Clinton that the distribution of wealth in the US became more skewed than it had at any time in the previous forty years. Inside the US under Clinton the ratio of wages for the average worker to the pay of the average CEO rose from 113 to 1 in 1991 to 449 to 1. Considering the difference between the richest and poorest 10 percent of humanity, inequality grew by 19 percent; by 77 percent, if you take the richest and poorest one percent.

The basic picture? "Under the full eight years of Clinton's presidency, even with the bubble ratcheting up both business investment and consumption by the rich, average real wages remained at a level 10 percent below that of the Nixon-Ford peak period, even though productivity in the economy was 50 percent higher under Clinton than under Nixon and Ford. The poverty rate through Clinton's term was only slightly better than the dismal performance attained during the Reagan-Bush years." We had a bubble boom, pushed along by consumer spending by the rich.

Speculative rampages were given a green light.

To be sure, in accord with the captious laws of class-based mechanics, the bubbling tide did raise boats, albeit unevenly. The yachts of the rich lofted magnificently on the flood. Meaner skiffs rose an inch or two. In those bubble years businesses needed more workers, and for a brief moment the labor shortage gave them some leverage to get more pay.

Nowhere is Pollin more persuasive than in analyzing the causes of the fiscal turnaround from deficit to surplus, an achievement that had Al Gore in 2000 pledging to pay down the entire federal debt of $5.8 trillion. Was this turnaround the consequence of economic growth (producing higher tax revenues), along with the moderate rise in marginal tax rates on the rich in 1993? If indeed these were the causes of fiscal virtue, we might take a benign view of Clinton's fiscal policies. On the other hand, if surplus was achieved by dint of hacking away at social expenditures and at social safety nets, plus gains in capital gains revenues stemming from the stock market bubble, then progressives, even Democratic candidates, might not so eagerly extol the Clinton model.

In a piece of original and trenchant analysis Pollin shows that almost two thirds of Clinton's fiscal turnaround can be accounted for by slashes in government spending relative to GDP (54 percent) and on capital gains revenues (10 percent). Pollin then asks the question. Suppose there really had been a peace dividend after the cold war was won? We could have had a few less weapons systems, 100,000 new teachers, 560,000 more scholarships, 1,400 new high schools and still had a budget surplus of $220 billion.

Wall Street applauded the surpluses and the ordinary folk paid the costs of all those slashes in the budget: fewer teachers, a dirtier environment.

You think the next Democratic nominee is going to address the long and short-term horrors engendered by the neoliberal credo to which Clinton paid such fealty? Of course not. What, at minimum, would have to be done? Pollin doesn't shirk the questions, and he suggests answers that steer past easy rhetorical flourishes about trade protections. If we are to move towards a world in which families don't have to line up outside churches to stay alive and teenagers don't have to work for 20 cents a day in Third World sweatshops, we have to have policies here that promote full employment and income security.

Such policies would have to include a strengthening of workers' legal rights to organize and to form unions; and also to fight on a level playing field in the conduct of strikes. To get a measure of fairness and stability in the financial system financial institutions would have to honor asset-based reserve requirements, of which one example would be the margin requirements Greenspan failed to impose in September, 1996. This same policy instrument could be used to channel credit to socially beneficial projects such as low income housing.

Despite the best efforts of our doctrinal leaders, the moral sentiments of the people are not entirely corrupted. Consumers, for example, are prepared to pay a premium if they can be assured they are buying products not made in sweatshops. And third-world countries need not survive only under the sweatshop conditions praised by Krugman and his colleague at the *Times*, Nicholas Kristof ("tremendous good news"). They have to be permitted to return to the somewhat protected conditions encouraged in the development policies of an earlier era, without agencies of the US government decreeing that their reformers and their union organizers be murdered by death squads.

For the millions of progressives who abandoned Al Gore in 2000 and either stayed at home or voted for Ralph Nader, what did the prospective Democratic nominee, John Kerry, offer?

By announcing April 9, 2004, that as president he would make deficit-reduction his prime task in managing the economy, Kerry as good as stated that he had no plans to combat America's greatest domestic problem: the lack of jobs, as advertised in the notorious "jobless recovery".

> As of the figures for April, 2003, more than two years into the recovery from the 2001 recession, the US economy had not produced any net increase in jobs – the first time since 1949 that this normal pattern of job growth in a recovery had not occurred.

Kerry had no plans to confront this crisis. His sole bet was on deficit reduction providing a decisive boost to the economy, and there's nothing to back up that theory, beyond the self-esteem of Kerry's economic team of ex-Clintonites.

Welcome back, Robert Rubin, the man who ran Clinton's economic policy on behalf of Wall Street. Kerry's economic advisers, Roger Altman and Gene Sperling, acknowledged in the late spring of 2004 they consulted with Rubin all the time.

Deficit reduction will do nothing to directly promote the growth of jobs, the lack of which is now the fundamental problem in the economy. As Pollin remarks, "It is also a political disaster for the Democrats to again latch onto deficit reduction rather than jobs as their major economic theme. The false premise of Rubinomics is that deficit reduction itself promotes economic growth, and thereby jobs, by lowering long-term interest rates. This is what Rubin and company think happened in the 1990s. But they are wrong. What actually happened in the 1990s is that we had an unprecedented stock market bubble. Because of the bubble, rich people and corporations engaged in a huge wave of borrowing and spending that drove the economy upward, only to crash back down when the bubble collapsed."

Even if Rubin were right about deficit reduction stimulating growth of GDP, what is clear in the current "recovery" is that GDP growth alone does not promote job growth. That is exactly what we mean by the "jobless recovery". The Democrats should instead be talking about a major jobs program, through refinancing state and local government spending in education, health, and social welfare. Aside from the social benefits from these programs, they also provide the biggest expansion of jobs for a given dollar amount of spending. A million dollars spent on education, Pollin calculates, would produce roughly twice the number of jobs as the same amount spent on the military.

But Kerry's other shoe, war on the deficit as well as war in Iraq, had a more sinister import. Deficits aren't intrinsically bad, and the current one is scarcely unparalleled in recent US economic history. But Bush's deficits, amassed in the cause of tax breaks for the very rich and war abroad, provide the premise of a fiscal crisis to starve social spending. It's the Greenspan Two Step: endorse the tax cuts, then say, as the Fed chairman did in February, that the consequent deficits require an onslaught on social security. Remember, Bill Clinton was all set to start privatizing social security, until the allurements of the divine Monica postponed the onslaught.

There are progressive ways to close the deficit. For example, Pollin reckons that if we imposed a very small tax on all financial transactions – i.e. all stock, bond, and derivative trades, starting with a 0.5 percent tax on stocks and scaling appropriately – we could raise roughly $100 billion right there, or roughly 20 percent of next year's projected deficit, even if we also assume financial market trading fell by an implausibly large 50 percent as a result of the tax.

A tax on financial transactions? Now you're talking, but not about anything you might expect from the Democratic Party or John Kerry.

The bottom line belongs to Karl Polanyi who argued in his 1944 masterpiece *The Great Transformation*, written amidst the Great Depression of the 1930s, that (in Pollin's explication) "for market economies to function with some modicum of fairness, they must be embedded in social norms and institutions that effectively promote broadly accepted notions of the common good. Otherwise, acquisitiveness and competition – the two driving forces of market economies – achieve overwhelming dominance as cultural forces".

Chapter 3

"We can thank Monica Lewinsky for the fact that Social Security was not handed over to the mutual funds industry by Clinton and the Democrats."

Robin Blackburn
How Monica Lewinsky Saved Social Security

ROBIN BLACKBURN

How Monica Lewinsky
Saved Social Security

HAD IT NOT BEEN FOR MONICA'S CAPTIVATING SMILE and first inviting snap of that famous thong, President Bill Clinton would have consummated the politics of triangulation, heeding the counsel of a secret White House team and deputy treasury secretary Larry Summers. Late in 1998 or in the State of the Union message of 1999 a solemn Clinton would have told Congress and the nation that, just like welfare, Social Security was near-broke, had to be "reformed" and its immense pool of capital tendered in part to the mutual funds industry. The itinerary mapped out for Clinton by the Democratic Leadership Committee would have been complete.

It was a desperately close run thing. On the account of members of Clinton's secret White House team, mandated to map out the privatization path for Social Security, they had got as far down the road as fine-tuning the account numbers for Social Security accounts now released to the captious mercies of Wall Street. But in 1998 the Lewinsky scandal burst upon the President, and as the months sped by and impeachment swelled from a remote specter to a looming reality, Clinton's polls told him that his only hope was to nourish the widespread popular dislike for the hoity-toity elites intoning Clinton's death warrant.

In an instant Clinton spun on the dime and became Social Security's mighty champion, coining the slogan "Save Social Security First".

LET US NOW RECONSTRUCT THE PLOT IN GREATER DETAIL.

In the mid-1990s pessimism about the future of Social Security was rife in seminars, conferences, op-eds and learned papers by which elite consensus is fashioned. The media lent an eager ear to charlatanry from outfits like the Third Millennium, which ventriloquized a supposed consensus amongst youth that the program would not be there for them when they came to retire – and that consequently their best bet was to take their FICA payments and put them in a private share account in soar-away Wall Street. Third Millennium released artfully contrived polls claiming to show that, for example, more young Americans believed in UFOs than in the future of Social Security. In fact the poll had no question linking the two propositions but this didn't stop lazy columnists and editorialists from picking it up and kindred 'findings' such as that *General Hospital* would outlast the program or that a bet on the Super Bowl was a more rational use of money.

Third Millennium was, of course, a front for the privatization lobby. But it did tap into a vein of public anxiety and skepticism concerning Social Security finances and, with the stock market soaring upward, its Wall Street connections were an asset not a liability. Whatever the exaggerations of the privatizers, the claim that an aging society would have to meet rising costs was not in itself wrong. The idea that "something must be done" was widespread and many expected that Clinton would follow up his capitulation to Republicans on welfare with a deal on Social Security. But he didn't, thanks to the zaftig young woman in a blue dress who caught his eye in 1995.

We have this on the authority of high-ranking members of the Clinton Treasury who gathered in Harvard in the summer of 2001 to mull over the lessons of the 1990s. At that conclave it was revealed that on Clinton's orders a top secret White House working party had been established to study in detail the basis for a bipartisan policy on Social Security that would splice individual accounts into the program. Such was the delicacy of this exercise that meetings of the group were flagged under the innocent rubric "Special Issues" on the White House agenda.

What was in fact being prepared for the President was precisely that second dose of welfare reform, this time targeted on the very citadel of the New Deal, the Social Security program Roosevelt himself established.

The "Special Issues" secret team was set up by then-Deputy Treasury Secretary Larry Summers (later elevated to Treasury Secretary and now President of Harvard) and Gene Sperling, the head of the Council of Economic Advisers. The Deputy Treasury Secretary's fondness for schemes to privatize Social Security comes as no surprise. As chief economist of the World Bank in the early 1990s Summers had commissioned a notorious report, "Averting the Old Age Crisis", that argued that Merrill Lynch and Fidelity would be better at pension provision than any government. In fact governments should offer only a safety net and farm out their power to tax payrolls to private financial concerns, which would run mandatory funded pensions on the Chilean model. The task of the Special Issues group was to find an installment of privatization that could reconcile realistic Republicans and Democrats, and be sold as still honoring most existing entitlements.

Participants at the Harvard conference conceded that severe technical problems beset efforts to introduce commercial practices. The existing program has low administration costs whereas running tens of millions of small investment accounts would be expensive. The secret White House team sought to finesse the problem by pooling individual funds and stripping down the element of choice or customer service. But Summers was unhappy: as one team member now recalls it, "Deputy Secretary Summers was fond of saying that we had to guard against the risk of setting up the Post Office when people were used to dealing with Federal Express". And pooled funds were also to be avoided because they would risk government control of business.

Some members of the team also worried that allowing employees the option of setting up their own accounts would soon turn into a "slippery slope", since the defection of the richest five or ten per cent of employees would soon undermine the program's ability to honor its commitments to existing retirees.

Nevertheless, under Summers' guidance, the secret team pushed forward. There were high hopes that the President would embrace what had by now had become a detailed blueprint: "The working group's estimates were at the level of detail that it was determined how many digits an ID number would have to be for each fund and how many key strokes would therefore be required to enter all of the ID numbers each year."

Clinton was kept up to date with briefings every few weeks and in July 1998 attended one of the "Special Issues" meetings himself. But in that same month he was served with a grand jury subpoena. A month later he finally acknowledged a sexual relationship with Monica.

By the end of 1998 the secret team concluded with heavy hearts that the escalating Lewinsky affair might well doom all their efforts. The President was desirous to be seen doing something dramatic for Social Security, but not anything risky. It could be controversial, but controversial in the direction of doing more for the program, not endangering it. As one team member put it this summer in the Harvard conclave: "Toward the end of 1998, as the possibility that the President would be impeached came clearly into view, the policy dynamic of the Social Security debate changed dramatically and it became clear to the White House that this was not the time to take risks on the scale that would be necessary to achieve a deal on an issue as contentious as Social Security reform."

Clinton was so desperate for an approach that would prove popular that he was even prepared to disappoint Wall Street. "The President decided to follow a strategy of trying to unite the

Democrats around a plan that would strengthen Social Security by transferring budget surpluses to Social Security and investing a portion in equities."

In his 1999 State of the Union address Clinton seized the initiative from the privatizers with a bold new plan that gave substance to the "Save Social Security First" slogan. He proposed that 62 per cent of the budget surplus should be used to build up the Social Security trust fund. He promised to veto any attempt to divert Social Security funds to other uses, and he urged that 15 per cent of the trust fund should be invested in the stock market, not by individuals but by the Social Security Administration.

Part of the cunning of this approach was that it stole a Republican theme. While rejecting individualization it insisted that Social Security funds should not be spent on other programs or on tax cuts. Republicans had urged that Social Security taxes be placed in a "lock box" and soon Clinton himself was using the term. Not content with this Clinton also offered public subsidies to Universal Savings Accounts that would be set up outside Social Security and not at its expense. This was a residue of the commercializing approach but it won few plaudits from the privatizers as it was a voluntary add-on to a strengthened public program.

Federal Reserve chairman Alan Greenspan was willing to see the budget surplus pledged to Social Security but he denounced the plan to invest the trust fund in equities on the grounds that it would lead to government interference in business. A writer in the *New York Times*, January 25, 1999, warned that if the trust fund was allowed to invest in stocks and shares it would be impossible to prevent the politicization of investment: "The danger is that Congress will meddle, for example, steering funds into environmentally-friendly companies rather than, say, tobacco companies." The next day Milton Friedman contributed an excited piece to the *Wall Street Journal* warning that Clinton was embarked on a different type of slippery slope to that pondered by his secret team: "I have often speculated that an ingenious way for a socialist to achieve his objective would be to persuade Congress, in the name of fiscal responsibility, to (1) fully fund obligations under Social Security and (2) invest the accumulated reserves in the capital market by purchasing equity interests in domestic corporations." Clinton had promised that the trust fund would be insulated from political pressure and that only 15 per cent of the trust fund would be invested, but Friedman was not at all convinced.

Clinton was also attacked for "double counting" when he pledged the budget surplus for Social Security. But accounts at the Harvard conference make clear that this concerned the pledge about the surplus aimed at separating the trust fund from the rest of the Federal budget. The proposal to allow the trust to hold a range of assets, not simply Treasury IOUs, would not only give Social Security real assets but would also create a powerful new lever on economic policy, something that Greenspan was jealously aware of.

Despite such attacks the Clinton plan as a whole went down very well with the American people. Republicans were swiftly moved to insist that they too would give priority to Social Security. Pessimism about the future of the program was replaced by a growing consensus that the program must be – and could be – saved. All that was needed was the will and a determination not to squander the trust fund.

Under the lash of the Lewinsky crisis, a President had issued a full-throated endorsement of the Social Security system. It was a terrible blow to a spectrum of opinion that stretched from the Cato Institute and Third Millennium to many New Democrats, including Senator Joseph Lieberman, who has proclaimed the need for individual accounts in the name of "choice". In his presidential campaign Al Gore, we should note, publicly opposed the idea of the Social Security trust fund holding a range of assets.

Even the Republic leadership sheepishly rallied to the notion that the surplus on the Social Security fund should be spent on nothing else. Just four days before the election George W. Bush told a crowd in Saginaw, Michigan, that protecting the Social Security trust fund was going to be one of his top priorities. The employee's Social Security taxes, he promised, were "only going to be spent on one thing – what they're meant for – Social Security. We're not going to let Congress touch them for any other reason." Less than a year later the Congressional Budget Office forecast that the administration would need $9 billion from the Social Security Trust Fund to balance its budget and much more next, even as Bush reassured Democratic Senate Majority leader Tom Daschle that he wouldn't raid the famous Social Security lock-box.

Bush's predicament over the trust fund was the more edgy because he wanted to introduce individual accounts into Social Security and has set up his own Commission to work out the best way to deliver this taste of privatization. The Bush White House web site featured an explanation of the promised "reform" which fulsomely insisted that all Social Security must be respected and that the private accounts would not be allowed to jeopardize them in any way.

The Democrats can blame the President for creating the budget problem by an unwise tax cut. If they had the guts the Democrats could have found a strategy for economic recovery by revisiting the Social Security debate of the late nineties, when Clinton not only coined the slogan now giving grief to his successor – 'Save Social Security First' – but also boldly proposed separating the trust fund from the federal budget, allowing the trustees to pursue an investment strategy of its own.

The logic of Social Security was once memorably explained and defended by Larry Summers' brilliant uncle, the Nobel laureate Paul Samuelson. Compulsory social arrangements of this sort were, he explained, a necessary defense against greedy and short-sighted "free riders"; "if all but one obey, the one may gain selfish advantage by disobeying - which is where the sheriff comes in: we politically invoke force on *ourselves*.... Once social coercion or contracting is admitted into the picture the ... problem (of free riders) disappears." Samuelson was impelled to show that individualism needs collectivism: "That the Protestant ethic should have been instrumental in creating individualistic capitalism one may accept: but that it should stop there is not necessarily plausible. What made Jeremy Bentham a Benthamite in 1800, one suspects, might in 1900 have made him a Fabian (and do we not see a lot in common in the personalities of James Mill and Friedrich Engels?)... Let mankind enter into a Hobbes-Rousseau social contract in which the young are assured of their retirement subsistence if they will today support the aged, such assurance to be guaranteed by a draft on the yet unborn." (This passage is to be found in Samuelson's paper, "An Exact Consumption-Loan Model of Interest with or without the Social Contrivance of Money", *Journal of Political Economy*, December 1958.)

But by 1998 Samuelson's nephew, Larry Summers, was busy undermining the social contract between the generations and, as we have seen, it took young Lewinsky to give it extra breathing space. In the process the Clinton White House, mired in scandal as it was, found itself exploring ideas of collective funding that went beyond the pay-as-you-go principles that Samuelson enunciated. If generations are of unequal size, and if the aging of the population gives rise to increased retirement or medical costs, then it becomes wise to introduce an element of pre-funding. Clinton and Gore eventually settled on a strategy of using such a fund to pay down the public debt and invoking the "lock box". But the papers at that Harvard conference showed that sooner or later pre-funding could not be confined to paying down the public debt, partly because surpluses might swallow it up in a few years and partly because it might not be feasible or advisable to do so.

The Harvard papers were not the only evidence of new thinking on Social Security in the wake of the impeachment crisis. In another part of the Clinton White House an aide called Peter Orszag was working with Joseph Stiglitz, then Chief Economist at the World Bank, on a paper entitled "Rethinking Pension Reform: Ten Myths about Social Security Systems". This constituted a powerful critique of the earlier World Bank report commissioned by Summers. The paper, originally delivered in September 1999, was later published in a book edited by Robert Holzman and Stiglitz, entitled *New Ideas About Old Age Security*. Its whole thrust is to defend public provision and to explore forms of pre-funding that would assist this. Indeed the paper, several of whose points are born out by the difficulties encountered by Clinton's secret team, now give the opponents of privatization a potent weapon.

The collapse of the markets at the end of the Nineties bubble also meant that Bush and his Commission had a much harder task ahead of them, before the focus of terrorism changed the whole focus of Bush's agenda. Flawed as it is, the case for privatization was superficially appealing during the heady days of the late-1990s bull market. Indeed its defeat at that time could turn out to have been decisive. On the other hand the economic downturn makes more relevant than ever the other prong of the original Clinton strategy, namely the idea that the Trust Fund should acquire its own assets. In a recession-hit economy these could include public bonds linked to investment in education or urban renewal, or they could involve injecting funds into sectors downcast by post-bubble blues. This would, it is true, be to go further than Clinton ever suggested – but it would be fully in the spirit of many left proponents of the original trust fund when it was added to the program in 1939 and it would be very well received by many sections of organized labor, such as the folks at the Heartland Alliance.

In his famous book *What is History?* E.H. Carr debated the influence on history exercised by Cleopatra's nose. Future historians of Social Security will be able to intersperse their explanation of the intricacies of COLAS, bend points and IPEs with at least a paragraph on the political and intellectual consequences of Monica's beguiling smile. She saved the day.

Chapter 4

"By early fall of 1996 it was clear the Democrats had a chance of regaining the House. Would not that recapture afford a better chance of crafting a welfare bill not compromised by Gingrich and the others? To this day many Democrats in Congress become incensed on the topic of what Clinton and Gore did. On the eve of a Democratic convention, with Gingrich already ensconced in the national imagination as the Bad Guy, Clinton had just made common cause with him, thus undercutting all plans to campaign against the Gingrich Congress."

Alexander Cockburn and Jeffrey St. Clair
War on the Poor

ALEXANDER COCKBURN AND JEFFREY ST. CLAIR
War on the Poor

IN NOVEMBER OF 1994 TWO YEARS OF RAMSHACKLE government, breached pledges and the Clinton administration's frequently manifested contempt for its traditional base, exacted their price. In the midterm elections Republicans seized control of both the House and the Senate for the first time since the Eisenhower era. The rout extended to governors' mansions across the country, where the Republicans captured the majority of governorships for the first time in a quarter-century. Newt Gingrich, the new Speaker of the House, became the nation's political wunderkind.

Yet for Bill Clinton the Democratic defeat held its paradoxical allure. The old-line Democratic congressional leadership no longer held sway on the Hill. Tom Foley and Dan Rostenkowski were gone altogether – one back to the Inland Empire of the Pacific Northwest and the other to a federal penitentiary. The White House no longer had to dicker with hostility to its agenda from New Deal-oriented Democrats. Without the threat of a presidential veto to lend clout to their resistance, the liberal Democrats on the Hill were impotent against the Republicans flourishing their Contract with America. Thus unencumbered, the Clinton administration could cut deals with the Republican leadership.

All this strategy needed was a name, and soon after the election Clinton summoned in the man who would introduce "triangulation" into the lexicon of the late 1990s.

Dick Morris, a man of elastic political scruple, had enjoyed a fluctuating relationship with Clinton. He'd bailed out the young governor of Arkansas after the latter's first comeuppance at the hands of the voters in 1980. Since then Morris had served many masters, ranging from the millionaire socialist from Ohio,

Howard Metzenbaum, to Bella Abzug of New York, to Trent Lott of Mississippi ("I love his feisty, shit-on-the-shoes style") and Jesse Helms of North Carolina. Morris worked as a consultant for Helms in 1990, in a particularly foul campaign against the black Democratic challenger, Harvey Gantt.

Morris came to the White House with the purpose of providing new ideas and a new strategy. He says Clinton told him, "I've lost confidence in my current team." Morris commenced his mission of refreshment under conditions of secrecy, codenamed Charlie, his function at first known only to the Clintons. His advice: steal the Republicans' thunder, draw down the deficit, reform welfare, cut back government regulation and "use Gore's reinventing government program to cut the public sector's size." The president should demonstrate toughness, Morris counseled, with decisive action overseas.

As the new Republican leadership took over in January of 1995, Clinton summoned Gore to the Oval Office, disclosed the hiring of Morris and instructed the vice president to work with him. "Charlie" then laid out the new agenda for Gore. Morris later wrote, "He grasped what I was saying at once and offered his full support...Gore told me that he had been increasingly troubled by the drift of the White House...He said he had tried, in vain, to move the administration toward the center, but the White House staff had shut him out...Gore said, 'We need a change here, a big change, and I'm hoping and praying that you're the man to bring it.' We shook hands on our alliance."

Soon Morris, Gore and Clinton came to two fateful decisions. As part of the strategy of stealing the Republicans' thunder, Morris urged an intensive fundraising drive, aimed at amassing "soft money" for TV spots designed to boost the new Clinton agenda, trump the Republicans and detour the old-line concerns of the Democrats at the other end of Pennsylvania Avenue. Soft money earns that much-abused name because it can be raised in amounts not limited by campaign spending laws; it can be procured directly from corporations, labor unions or other institutions so long as the money is used to promote "issues" rather than specific candidates. That at least is how the law supposed soft money would work. Morris knew very well that the issue ads would be identified directly with Clinton, because they would sound themes Morris himself had prescribed. To execute these ads Morris and Gore turned to the latter's longtime media consultant, Bob Squier. Down the road lay many a funding scandal, not least the Buddhist temple imbroglio that found Al Gore on the receiving end of thousands of dollars in contributions from monks and nuns supposedly ennobled by the spiritual distinction of poverty. But such things were still a year away.

The time had come to go public with the new line. Morris drafted a speech for Clinton in which the president would announce that he was ready to work with the Republicans. It laid out the grounds on which the President was prepared to meet Newt Gingrich. Within the White House there was a storm of protest, led by Leon Panetta, Clinton's chief of staff and onetime California congressman, who was aghast at what he correctly perceived to be the betrayal of his former colleagues on the Hill.

As Panetta presented his case, Clinton began to tilt toward his position. Morris sensed crisis at hand. At the crucial moment, so he relates, Gore, who had been silently following the debate, made a decisive intervention. "I agree with Dick's point, that we need to emerge from the shadows and place ourselves at the center of the debate with the Republicans by articulating what we will accept and what we will not in a clear and independent way." It was music to Morris's ears, and he cried, "Bravo!"

For Morris, as for his employer, polls were everything. He developed what he called a "neuro-psychological profile" of the American voter, and established an iron rule that no initiative could be undertaken by the White House unless polling showed an approval rating of 60 percent. By constant polling he concocted what he called a "values agenda". At the top of the list was affirmative action. "Mend it, don't end it" was the mantra, which meant, in practice, destroy affirmative action from the inside while professing support for the general principle.

Next came TV violence. Intimidate the networks, Morris advised, into adopting a "voluntary" system of ratings for TV shows and movies. Soon media executives were summoned to the White House for a session with Clinton and Gore. Simultaneously Clinton pushed for installation of the so-called V-chip in all new TV sets, which would allow parents to block all offensive material. Next came teen pregnancy, an issue pounded on by the Clinton White House, even though the rate had been falling. Education: go after tenured teachers, an attack increasingly popular in Morris's focus groups, and demand that at least they be tested. Youth: advocate school uniforms and curfews for teens. Gay marriage: on Morris's advice Clinton and Gore embraced the Defense of Marriage Act, a purely grandstanding piece of legislation which preemptively bars gay marriages from recognition under federal law for any purpose. Immigration: the poll numbers were off the chart, and the Clinton White House duly set a goal to double the number of turn-backs by the Immigration and Naturalization Service – among other things, enlisting the Labor Department to help speed the pace and breadth of workplace raids. Taxes: Morris believed that Main Street America was now playing the market, so that a 20 percent reduction in the capital gains tax rate would be hugely popular.

But there were two issues that towered above the rest in Morris's assaying of public opinion: welfare and crime. In the 1992 campaign, Clinton had pledged to "end welfare as we know it." In 1993, Gore had urged Clinton to declare war on welfare as part of the first 100 days and had implored the president to let him lead the charge. After all, Gore argued, he was one of the few Democratic senators to have supported a welfare-to-work law narrowly approved in 1988, forcing states to require parents getting welfare checks to work at least 16 hours per week in unpaid jobs. But Hillary thought an attack on welfare would divert energy from her health care package, and Gore lost the battle.

By 1995 the welfare rolls were shrinking, from a peak of 18 million in the recession of 1991 to about 12.8 million. Defenders of the system in Clinton's cabinet, Labor Secretary Robert Reich and Donna Shalala of Health and Human Services, argued that the total budget for Aid to Families with Dependent Children was a tiny fraction of the federal budget; indeed, it was only 14 percent of the amount devoted to Medicare, a middle-class entitlement. The real problem, they argued, was lack of training for the chronically underemployed and unemployed.

Reflexively hostile to welfare and fortified by Morris's polls, Clinton pressed ahead. The administration began granting waivers to states to implement their own onslaughts on welfare, feature "workfare" requirements, time limits and "family caps", a punishment for women who dared to have more than the approved number of children the government would help support. Through 1995 and early in 1996 the Republicans had passed and sent to Clinton two bills to dismantle the federal welfare system. He vetoed both, but in his veto messages he stressed that he agreed with much of their content in principle. Peter Edelman, a high level official at HHS, described this as "the squeeze play", whereby Clinton would reap approval from Democratic New Dealers for standing up for poor kids while at the same time signaling that in the long run he'd throw the mothers of those kids off the rolls altogether.

As they approached the Democratic convention in the summer of 1996, Clinton was floating on Morris's magic carpet. Assisted by staggering blunders by Gingrich and a lackluster opponent in Bob Dole, Clinton was ahead by no less than 27 percent in the polls. The Republicans were eager to wrap up their legislative work before the conventions in July and August. They pushed through a welfare bill arguably worse than the ones Clinton had vetoed previously. Many Democrats on the Hill believed that Clinton would veto this bill too. But Senator Daniel Patrick Moynihan of New York had more sensitive political antennae. He warned, "I've heard that the leaders of the cabinet recommended a veto but that the president remains under the sway of his pollsters."

On July 30, 1996, Clinton mustered his cabinet to hear arguments on whether or not he should sign the Republicans' bill. One by one his advisers said he should not. No's from people like Shalala and Reich came as no surprise. But similarly disapproving were not only Leon Panetta but Laura Tyson, his chief economic adviser, Henry Cisneros of HUD and even Treasury Secretary Robert Rubin, who said that too many people would be harmed by the bill and that it show an act of political courage to veto it.

Not trusting Shalala's department to produce objective assessments of the consequences of the bill, the White House staff had commissioned a survey from the Urban Institute, a DC think tank. The numbers were dire. The bill would push 2.6 million people further into poverty – 1.1 million of them children. In all, the Institute predicted that 11 million families would lose income. That was the best-case scenario. In the event of a recession (which would come in 1993), the numbers would be far, far worse. In that fateful cabinet meeting Rubin invoked this study, and the numbers seemed to find their mark with Clinton, while Gore remained mute.

The meeting came to an end and Clinton, Panetta and Gore headed for the Oval Office for a private session. All accounts agree that, first, Panetta again made the case for a veto, laying particular emphasis on an appalling provision in the bill that would deny legal immigrants federal assistance, such as food stamps. Finally Gore broke his silence and urged Clinton to sign.

Clinton, Morris and Gore prepared a press statement, delivered by the president later that same day. Clinton admitted that the bill contained "serious flaws" but went on to say, "This is the best chance we will have in a long time to complete the work of ending welfare as we know it." No one at the press conference quizzed Clinton on this curious claim. After all, the election was only about three months away. By early fall of 1996 it was clear The Democrats had a chance of regaining the House. Would not that recapture afford a better chance of crafting a welfare bill not compromised by Gingrich and the others?

To this day many Democrats in Congress become incensed on the topic of what Clinton and Gore did. On the eve of a Democratic convention, with Gingrich already ensconced in the national imagination as the Bad Guy, Clinton had just made common cause with him, thus undercutting all plans to campaign against the Gingrich Congress. As for Al Gore the consensus was that he was looking ahead to a possible challenge in 2000 from his old rival Dick Gephardt. With Morris's polls showing that an attack on welfare scored well over the 60 percent bar, Gore would have the advantage over Gephardt or any other liberal challenger.

SUSPICIONS ABOUT GORE DEEPENED AS THE FALL CAMPAIGN proceeded. The president and vice president argued that it was crucial that they be re-elected so that they fix the problems with the welfare bill they had just signed. The problems here concerned not the welfare bill itself but the denial of federal services to legal immigrants and a slash in the food stamp program. In October of 1996, with the presidential election no longer in doubt, Democratic candidates came to the Democratic National Committee urgently seeking infusions of cash to help them in the crucial final weeks. Finally, Senator Christopher Dodd of Connecticut, then the general chairman of the DNC, organized a meeting with Clinton and Gore. Dodd explained that the two were home safe and there was a chance to recapture the House. Clinton seemed amenable to a release of funds. Gore adamantly disagreed. By one account, Gore was the only person in the White House to oppose this transfer of funds from the presidential campaign to congressional races. It's a measure of how a number of Democrats view Al Gore that some participants in that meeting felt that the only explanation for his conduct was that he did not want the Democrats to re-take control of the House because victory would elevate Gephardt to Speaker of the House.

The cynicism may not have stopped there. Why did Clinton and Gore decide to sign on to that third Republican welfare bill? The only major difference from the previous ones came in the form of the denial of federal services to legal immigrants and a $2.5 billion cut in the food stamp program. It's likely that these two Republican add-ons were what allured the White House, because (as noted above) Clinton could then turn to the liberals saying they needed him to be re-elected so he could repair part of the damage wrought by the very bill he had just signed. In fact the White House probably could have insisted the riders be dropped, because Dole desperately wanted a legislative victory under the Republicans' belt.

The welfare bill ended a federal entitlement that had been a cornerstone of the New Deal. It caps the federal contribution to welfare programs at $14.6 billion a year and hands the money over in block grants to the states to distribute as they see fit. The main requirement is that the states agree that welfare recipients can spend no more than a total of five years in their lifetime on welfare. It allows states to adopt even harsher standards. Finally, under the old system, welfare money came to the recipient as cash. Under the new system, the money can be given to intermediaries, for possible conversion to other services such as housing or food. Al Gore particularly liked this provision. In Atlanta in May of 1999, he told an audience why: "It allows faith-based organizations to provide basic welfare services. They can do so with public funds – without having to alter the religious character that is so often the key to their effectiveness. We should extend this approach to drug treatment, homelessness and youth violence prevention. People who work in faith-and values-based organizations are driven by their spiritual commitment. They have done what government can never do: provide compassionate care. Their client is not a number but a child of god." In other words, treat welfare payments like school vouchers. Gore had just laid out the welcome mat for Bush's faith-based initiatives.

Not long after Clinton signed the welfare bill, judgment came from Senator Moynihan, who had begun his service to the state back in the sixties with sermons about the "pathology" of the black family and now, bizarrely, was defending the system he'd denounced for years. Even this man of all seasons and all masters was shocked: "It is a social risk no sane person would take, and I mean that. If you think things can't get worse, just wait until there are a third of a million people on the streets... It's not welfare reform; it's welfare repeal."

Hugh Price, president of the National Urban League, called the bill "an abomination for America's most vulnerable mothers and children" and accused Clinton, Gore and the Congress of defecting from a war on poverty and "waging a war against poor people instead."

Within weeks three high-ranking officials in the Department of Health and Human Services had resigned: Mary Jo Bane, Walter Primus and Peter Edelman. That was it. Across the length and breadth of the Clinton administration, only these resignations were tendered in principle against this abandonment of the New Deal and the shafting of America's poor. Since that time Edelman has missed no opportunity to denounce the bill as a punitive strike against defenseless people. "The bill closes its eyes to all the facts and complexities of the real world and essentially says to recipients: find a job."

The edict "find a job" was central to the bill and to the mythology nourished by opponents of welfare—that freeloaders with jobs available to them were abusing the system. Of course, there is always some abuse, but study after study had shown that most welfare recipients had looked for jobs and couldn't find a suitable one or had been on welfare for a limited period, then found a job and got off the rolls. In 1999 a University of Michigan study making an assessment three years after the welfare bill went into effect found that the welfare population faces "unusually high barriers to work: such as physical and mental health problems, domestic violence and lack of transportation." More than 30 percent of the families on welfare are constrained by disability, a sick child, no child care or an infirm relative. Those that want to find work are faced with narrow options even in an economy hyped as in mid-boom. In 1996 the Congressional Budget Office offered some bleak realities about the reserve army of the unemployed. With an official unemployment rate of four percent (the unofficial rate is roughly twice that, since government figures don't count frustrated people who have given up looking for work), there are still three to five people needing work for each available job. In the Bush recession, this ratio rose to more than 10 to one.

In urban areas the job market is even more constricted. A 1998 study in Harlem showed just how brutally competitive the low-wage job market is. Over a five-month period, an average of fourteen people applied for each job opening at a local McDonalds. A year later researchers from the University of Chicago found that 73 percent of those same job searchers still hadn't found even minimum wage level work.

In many states, there's the last resort of workfare, which compels welfare recipients to accept public jobs, such as highway clean-up or garbage picking with the Parks

Department, in return for benefits. Nationally the average benefit for workfare jobs is $381 per month, which works out to $4.40 an hour, or 80 percent of the minimum wage. But in some places it's much worse. Mississippi, for example, requires single mothers to work twenty hours a week at $1.38 an hour, and a two-parent household to work fifty-five hours at 50 cents an hour.

On top of this the people in the workfare labor force are denied such basic rights as collective bargaining, unemployment insurance, the earned income tax credit and Social Security credit. States are finding it to their budgetary advantage to fill job vacancies with these "slavefare" workers. A Senate study in 1996 estimated that the consequences of welfare reform would depress the wages of the working poor by 12 percent.

Allowing the states to freelance their welfare programs has resulted in some particularly cruel policies and inequities. Minnesota spends $50 million a year on child care for single mothers receiving welfare benefits who are working or looking for work. New York spends $54 million to serve a population six times as large. Clinton and Gore repeatedly touted the approach taken by Indiana, where welfare reform was instituted by a Democratic governor, Evan Bayh, and his successor in the governor's mansion, Frank O'Bannon. The pair presided over the shrinking of the welfare rolls in the Hoosier state by 30 percent. There's no way to know if those people actually found work. It's possible that the conditions of supervision of welfare recipients simply became unbearable and they left the program and perhaps the state. Under Indiana's scheme, one missed job-training course means the loss of a welfare check for two months. A second infraction means loss of benefits for a year. A third strike and you're out for good.

The Clinton welfare bill also includes a provision that allows states to begin drug testing welfare recipients. In theory the provision was aimed at people suspected of having drug problems.

Oregon, for example, initiated a testing policy but soon reversed course when recipients began dropping out of the welfare program to avoid testing. The state found that it was better to stop drug testing, keep people in the program and steer addicts into treatment. Michigan took a different approach. In 1999 the state adopted a mandatory drug-testing policy for all welfare recipients, which prompted a lawsuit by the ACLU. A federal judge ruled in 1999 that the policy was unconstitutional. He noted that in the five weeks of the program's operation there were positive drug tests in only eight percent of the cases, and all but three of those were for marijuana.

In his 2000 campaign, Al Gore pushed for what he called "Welfare Reform 2", saying that more remained to be done to weed out cheats and freeloaders. He was particularly vehement in attacking dads behind on child support, vowing that he would make it easier for credit card companies to deny credit to such fathers. This would have come on top of a program, initiated by Janet Reno in her Florida years, whereby fathers behind on their payments get their driver's license lifted, meaning that they can't drive to work. In 1995, Clinton, Gore and Morris put into operation a program that saw these father's mug shots put up in Post Offices, their federal benefits garnished and the IRS sent on their trail. This pattern of inflicting administrative conviction outside the court system and due process is integral to the Clinton/Gore philosophy on crime.

The Clinton crime bill of 1994 introduced mandatory life imprisonment for persons convicted of a third felony in certain categories. It maintained the 100-to-1 disproportion in sentencing for crimes involving powder and crack cocaine, even though the US Sentencing Commission had concluded that the disparity was racist. It expanded to fifty the number of crimes that could draw the death penalty in a federal court, reaching even to crimes that did not include murders – the largest expansion of the death penalty in history. Pell grants giving prisoners an avenue to higher education were cut off. Federal judges were stripped of their powers to enforce the constitutional rights of prisoners and the power of states to set sentencing standards for drug crimes was greatly diminished.

The curtailment of states' rights went further. Grants for new prisons contained the provision that receipt of the money was dependent on the states ensuring that prisoners served at least 85 percent of their sentences. These inmates, remember, had been convicted in state, not federal, courts so this was simply federal blackmail to curtail parole at the state level. The Clinton administration also pressed the states to try juvenile offenders as adults. Gore articulated the administration's position: "When young people cross the line, they must be punished. When young people commit serious, violent crimes, they should be prosecuted like adults." Nonviolent offenders were to be sent to boot camps. Not, it should be noted, his own kids, who evaded punishment for nonviolent infractions such as smoking pot and having an open alcohol container in the car.

The Clinton/Gore administration was particularly assiduous in its assaults on the Fourth Amendment, protecting citizens against unreasonable searches and seizures. In 1994, they successfully pressed for a bill providing all communications providers to make existing and future communication systems wiretap ready. They also pushed hard for the so-called Clipper Chip, an encryption device that makes it easy for law enforcement and intelligence agencies to snoop on private messages.

The high-water mark in the Clinton administration's attack on the Bill of Rights came in 1996 with the Counter-Terrorism and Effective Death Penalty Act, which among other horrors allowed the INS to deport immigrants without due process, and denied prisoners the right to appeal to the federal bench based on habeas corpus petitions. "When historians write the story of civil liberties in the twentieth century," said Ira Glasser, head of the ACLU, "they will say that the Clinton administration adopted an agenda that has everything to do with weakening civil rights and nothing to do with combating terrorism."

In May of 2000, Gore outlined his campaign posture on crime and drugs in another speech in Atlanta. The erstwhile dope-smoker from Tennessee evidently feared that the man who refused to discuss cocaine use in his early years, George W. Bush, had the edge on the crime issue. Gore proclaimed he wanted to swaddle communities in "a blanket of blue". He swore that the minute he settled in the Oval Office, President Gore would call for 50,000 more cops (i.e., more half-trained recruits like the ones who shot Amadou Diallo forty-one times in the Bronx) and would allow off-duty cops to carry concealed weapons (which they almost all do anyway).

Gore promised prisoners what he called a simple deal: "Before you get out of jail you have to get clean. If you want to stay out, then you better stay clean. We have to stop that revolving door once and for all. First we have to test prisoners for drugs while they're in jail". Gore was so blithe in his disregard for elementary rights that he was unable to see a distinction between a prison sentence fully served and a further punitive add-on: "We have to insist on more prison time for those who don't break the habit". Even after prisoners are released the eye of the state would still follow them: "We should impose strict supervision on those who have just been released – and insist they obey the law and stay off drugs".

Another feature of Al Gore's prospective war on crime was the especially vigorous targeting of minority youth. "I will fight for a federal law that helps communities establish gang-free zones with curfews on specific gang members, a ban on gang-related clothing and the specific legal authority to break violent teen gangs once and for all".

Both parties have eagerly conjoined in militarizing the police, extending police powers and carving away basic rights. Often the Democrats have been worse. It was Republican

Representative Henry Hyde of Illinois who led the partially successful charge in 1999 against the seizure of assets in drug cases. It was Democrat Senator Charles Schumer of New York who played the role of factotum for the Justice Department in trying to head off Hyde and his coalition.

The rise of the Jackboot State has marched in lockstep with the insane and ineffective War on Drugs. This has been an entirely bipartisan affair. Its consequences are etched into the fabric of our lives. Just think of drug testing, now a virtually mandatory condition of employment, even though it's an outrageous violation of personal sovereignty, as well as being thoroughly unreliable. In an era in which America has been led by three self-confessed pot smokers – Clinton, Gore and Bush – the number of people held for drug crimes in federal prisons has increased by 64 percent.

No-knock raids are becoming more common as federal, state and local politicians and law enforcement agencies decide that the war on drugs justify dumping the Fourth Amendment. Even in states where search warrants require a knock on the door before entry, police routinely flout the requirement.

THE POSSE COMITATUS ACT FORBIDDING MILITARY INVOLVEment in domestic law enforcement is rapidly becoming as dead as the Fourth Amendment. Because of drug war exceptions created in that act, every region of the United States now has a Joint Task Force staff in charge of coordinating military involvement in domestic law enforcement. The involvement has now expanded to include anti-terrorism investigations.

In many cases, street deployment of paramilitary units is funded by "community policing" grants from the federal government. The majority of police departments use their paramilitary units to serve "dynamic entry" search warrants. The SWAT Team in Chapel Hill, North Carolina, conducted a large-scale crack raid of an entire block in a predominantly black neighborhood. The raid, termed Operation Redi-Rock, resulted in the detention and search of up to 100 people, all of whom were black. (Whites were allowed to leave the area.) No one was ever prosecuted for a crime. In Albany, New York, not long before the change-of-venue trial there of the four white cops who had killed Amadou Diallo in the Bronx, police in camouflage uniforms went on a ransacking spree in the black neighborhood of Arbor Hill, beating down doors house-to-house in search of a black suspect.

Where there is no social program, there's always a violence program. For the Clinton/Gore administration welfare reform and expansion of the police state were not only means to trump the Republicans; they were also essential to economic policy. Intense competition for jobs at the lowest rungs would depress wages, pit poor and working-class people against each other and, where workfare recipients displace municipal workers, weaken labor unions. The spectre and reality of incarceration would have the traditional effect of suppressing the dangerous classes, at a time when the wage gap between the rich and the poor grew wider than at any time in recent history.

Chapter 5

"I just have one question for the writers and feminist leaders who say we should vote for the Democratic candidate: do they want conditions for women in America to improve or do they want to get a Bush-lite Democrat into office? Because they should know by now that not only are these two roads not the same, not only do they not run parallel, they do not even exist on the same planet. One only needs to take a look at the troubling history of the Democratic Party and its neglect of women."

Brandy Baker
Women and the Democratic Party

BRANDY BAKER
Women and the Democratic Party

I DO NOT THINK THAT WE HUMANS FEEL ONLY ONE EMOTION at any given time. I had thought of the March For Women's Lives, Spring 2004, and I felt elated. Finally, the fight for women's reproductive rights was coming back out where it belongs: in the streets. But I also felt frustrated: why did it take the ban on the dilation and extraction procedure (the so-called "partial birth abortion" that eleven congressional Democrats voted for), the Bush administration's exploitation of Laci Peterson's awful murder, and John Ashcroft's snooping into women's medical records to galvanize the mainstream feminist leadership? None of this would have happened if a strong movement were in place to stop it. I could have just said "Better late than later" and have been happy about the Sunday demonstration if I wasn't so apprehensive. I knew that many liberals at the march would use this event as a soapbox to get out the vote for John Kerry: Bush-lite.

And they did.

War criminal Madeline Albright was welcomed with cheers, but the loudest applause went to Hillary Clinton with many shouting, "Hillary for president". And of course, accusations of "egomaniac" were thrown at Ralph Nader by many of the celebrities.

But what was disturbing is that after all of this time, liberal feminists were, and are, still relying on the same old electoral strategy to keep *Roe v. Wade*, and to keep the status quo.

There was no reason to suspect that the march would be anything other than a husting for the Democratic Party since 2004 was an election year and much of the ABB (Anybody But Bush) crowd had already been seeking ways to get the vote out for Kerry. Women's Voices, Women's Vote [WVWV], founded in

December 2003, is a "project to determine how to increase the share of unmarried women in the electorate and develop a set of messages to motivate their participation". WVWV was founded after pollsters Stanley Greenberg and Celinda Lake discovered an electoral goldmine for Democrats in the single woman demographic; they have a tendency to be politically progressive, yet noticeably absent on Election Day. Wonder why?

Since WVWV was established, scores of liberal writers had been whooping and hollering over the idea of this organization showing us single women the way to the polls so we can elect the Democratic Party's current Great White Father, John Kerry to the Big White House.

In her March, 2004, *Common Dreams* article, "A Different W: Move Over NASCAR Dads, the Sex and the City Crowd Could Turn the Election", Martha Burke suggested that in order not to "scare men", the Democrats should be "clever" by appealing "to men at the same time by saying: 'Just think how much better off every family would be if our daughters, mothers, and spouses were paid what they're worth.'" So Burke recommended that Kerry ask our fathers, boyfriends, and other males in our lives permission to court us. And why so little faith in the men in our lives and so much faith in these men who make up the Democratic Party establishment?

Katha Pollitt of *The Nation* did a little bit better. Not only did she point out the absurdity of the "Sex and the City Crowd" label for a group who are "disproportionately young, mobile, struggling and/or very, very poor" but she called for the Democrats to "come up with similar lures for the votes of single women – a federal living wage, universal public preschool and after-school (don't forget, singles with kids don't have the luxury of staying home with them), heck, free birth control".

In addition to abortion rights, these are also much needed reforms. We need a true women's movement that encompasses all of these concerns and more. But I just have one question for the writers and feminist leaders who say we should vote for Kerry: do they want conditions for women in America to improve or do they want to get a Bush-lite Democrat into office? Because they should know by now that not only are these two roads not the same, not only do they not parallel, they do not even exist on the same planet. One only needs to take a look at the troubling history of the Democratic Party and its neglect of women.

In 1980, for the first time, women voters outnumbered male voters, and feminists in the Democratic Party threatened to abandon Jimmy Carter and support independent presidential candidate John Anderson if the Democrats did not take women's issues seriously. This prospect got choice, ERA, and child care on the agenda.

In 1988, after eight brutal years of Reaganomics in which domestic programs were stripped of billions of dollars, there was a 24 percent gender gap in the pre-election polls in favor of Michael Dukakis.

It was single women, whether unwed, divorced, or widowed, who contributed most dramatically to the gap, along with working, educated, professional, young, and black women, who most supported a feminist agenda of pay equity, social equity, and reproductive rights.

Dukakis intentionally ignored women's issues, so the gap was reduced to eight points by Election Day. Despite GOP claims that Bush/Quayle had "narrowed the gender gap", the reality was that the Bush/Quayle ticket only received 50 percent of the women's vote. Obviously, many women felt that both parties were out of touch and stayed home.

With the promise of health care and education for all, and a country that wanted an end to the recession and twelve years of Reaganomics, Bill Clinton defeated George H.W. Bush in 1992. After his first year in office, Clinton abandoned health care reform along with his promises to make education more accessible to poor and working Americans. And on August 23, 1996, he signed the bill into law that dismantled welfare, a savage blow to many women and children in poverty.

Clinton successfully played on the racist fears of many Americans who put a black face to the media's caricatured welfare mother, when two thirds of the people on welfare were white. He took shots at the country's weakest citizens and played off the middle class against the poor by praising those who "work hard and play by the rules" and bragging that he wanted to end "welfare as we know it". He did nothing to try to get the Freedom of Choice Act passed, and admitted that he would have signed a "partial birth" abortion ban of his own if it made an exception. As the *New York Times* put it before the 1996 presidential election: "To be sure, the words change, and so do the ideas. Four years ago, Mr. Clinton spoke of providing health insurance to all Americans and expanding education and training to equip workers for a global economy. Now he talks of 48-hour hospital stays for mothers and newborns and uniforms for schoolchildren."

Three quarters of single women in America make under $50,000 a year. Almost a third of single women make less than $15,000 a year! But the key players in the mainstream feminist movement are perched much higher on the salary scale. This may explain their silence and inaction on Clinton's attacks on the poor, of which two thirds of are women. Clinton's policies did not affect the key players. And while many in the middle class feminist movement have graduated from the most elite schools in the nation, only 18 per cent of single women have a bachelor's degree or above. Law professor Anita Hill was embraced by the feminist movement when she came forward with her sexual harassment claims while Paula Jones, who possesses a high school education, was ridiculed.

Al Gore was a driving force behind welfare "reform". He hired Naomi Wolf to help him find his "inner alpha male" and pick his earth-toned wardrobe. Wolf later denied this, saying that she was in charge of writing memos on women's issues. Either she was paid for doing nothing at all, or those memos went into the trash. For his 2000 bid for the presidency, Gore offered women nothing more than a few words of lip service to the pro-choice position that he had only adopted in recent years (in 1991, Gore stated that abortion "was the taking of an innocent life"). He attacked Bill Bradley in the Democratic primary for calling for universal health care. Those millions of Americans who are uninsured are disproportionately women, and could have benefited from Clinton's promise for health care for all. And even during the Clinton years, abortion providers were not available in over 85 percent of all US counties: while the third of the country's single women who make under $15,000 per year may be not able to afford transportation to those few counties that have abortion providers, this lack of access would not be an issue for most liberal feminists. The reality is this: reproductive freedom will not be available to all women in the United States until we have universal health care.

During the 2000 presidential election, many feminists viciously attacked Ralph Nader for running for president as a Green Party candidate, despite feminism being one of the party's key principles. Nader, who has always been strong on economic issues, has always been a moderate on social issues. In his 2000 campaign, with a strong coalition of Left groups and individuals, he became more vocal on progressive concerns such as the death penalty, racial profiling, and privatized prisons. Nader is not perfect, and he did err with his claim that if *Roe v. Wade* were overturned the issue would go to the states (this would not be good for women in Louisiana), but Nader did what Clinton did not do, what Gore did not do, and what Kerry is not going to do: he listened to his constituency and adopted progressive issues that were not his primary focus before his 2000 run. As Nader himself said: "I've fought for women's rights since the 1950s.

I've been a leader in documenting marketplace discrimination against women that jeopardizes their health, safety, and economic rights."

The thought of anti-abortion zealots winning appointments to the Supreme Court under a Bush presidency was the one factor that terrified many into staying the course with the Democratic Party in 2000. Voters, many with pinched noses and sick stomachs, pulled the lever for Al Gore and the idea of *Roe v. Wade* being overturned has motivated many to support John Kerry's campaign this November.

On May 19, 2004, John Kerry told the Associated Press that he was open to the idea of appointing anti-abortion judges "as long as it doesn't lead to the Supreme Court overturning *Roe v. Wade*".

All hell would have broken loose if Ralph Nader had said something like this. The leaders of the feminist movement were ready to tar, feather, and run Nader out of DC when he blundered and proposed that if *Roe v. Wade* were overturned, abortion would be protected because the decision would go back to the states. But Elizabeth Cavendish, interim president of NARAL Pro-Choice America has only this to say about Kerry's statements: "There's a huge difference between Bush and Kerry on choice and this is not going to undermine the pages-long documentation that Kerry is pro-choice". Yes, Nader was wrong to say what he said in 2000, and no, he is not perfect, but what many do not know (and what the mainstream feminist movement will not tell you) is that Nader has signed on to NOW's platform of political, social, and economic rights for women. As of May, 2004, Kerry had not. And not long before Kerry told all of us that he was no redistribution Democrat, Nader spoke up for cleaning-people: a segment of the workforce that is overrepresented by women and people of color. Cleaning-people are noticed only when someone is unhappy with their work.

The problem is that we have a single issue women's movement that is not equipped to address the collective oppression of women who are on the lower rungs of the economic ladder because the movement restrains itself with blind support for the Democratic Party. Ralph Nader knows that abortion is not the only concern of the majority of this country's women, which is why he sticks up for those who clean the houses of the limousine liberals who are campaigning the hardest for Kerry.

Despite the fact that we won *Roe v. Wade* under the anti-choice Nixon administration and we did not have abortion providers in over 85 per cent of all counties under Clinton, many see a Democratic Party presidency as vital to securing abortion rights. John Kerry's statements killed the myth we are guaranteed pro-abortion judges if he becomes president; it also kills the other argument that ABBers have been promoting: you know, the one that claims that we can build a movement after we get a Democrat in office and that this Democrat will do all of the right stuff. Kerry said that he would be open to appointing anti-abortion judges to the Supreme Court only 24 days after what many have said was the largest demonstration in American history. Movements work; the two party system does not.

Like Nader, the feminist movement itself was once on the receiving end of invective about being splitters. In the summer of 1989, NOW delegates who were disgusted with the Democrats proposed an exploratory committee to discuss the possibility of launching a third party that would not only speak to specific women's issues, but would address militarism, racism, and poverty. After the media, which usually ignored NOW, castigated them for daring to toy with such an idea, feminist leaders publicly distanced themselves from the proposal. Again in 1992 NOW briefly considered the idea of forming a third party.

What happened to those days when we had standards: when we dreamed? Once upon a time, the feminists were actually considering breaking with the Democrats! Do you remember in the

1970s when women were talking about ERA, equal distribution of housework and child care? You do? Good, because I damn sure don't–seeing how I was born in the mid 1970s. But I remember hearing about these wonderful reforms and I remember hearing about women's liberation, I remember hearing about the radical critiques of these institutional structures that are built on racism, classism, and patriarchy. When women only seek to get seats at the table of the elites for themselves instead of dismantling that table, we get Hillary Clinton voting for the war in Iraq, Eleanor Smeal thanking Bush for bombing women in Afghanistan, and an upper middle class feminist movement that helps Democrats get in office and keeps a two party corporate system in power that hurts, not helps the majority of women and men in this society.

No reform was won by electing a Democrat. The Supreme Court passed *Roe v. Wade* in 1974 during the Nixon administration; the decision was written by Justice Harry Blackmun, a Nixon appointee. Nixon, an anti-choice right winger, was a war criminal, but when it came to domestic policy, he was this country's last progressive president. Now, Nixon was not a warm person known for his compassion. He was pushed by a movement that was on the ground, and it was not made up of politicians and lobbyists. It was comprised of people like the single women that the Democrats are trying to chase to the polls this November. All of the present Republican and Democratic senators voted for Scalia (including John Kerry): 98 out of 100. The two absentees were Republicans. Eleven Democrats voted for Clarence Thomas (52-48) in a then-Democratically controlled Senate. California, under Governor Ronald Reagan, was the first state to have legal abortions. Public support for the death penalty has dropped: that has been reflected in this current conservative Supreme Court's decision to ban executions of retarded people. This conservative court also upheld affirmative action policies in college admission and overturned the law that made sodomy in Texas illegal.

Now, as Bush seeks to corrode the one square foot of ground that we stand tiptoed on, we have a tougher fight because there wasn't a battle for more when we had two square feet: just a battle in Congress by professional lobbyists to keep what little we had, and if it was chipped away by Democrats we were supposed to look away and pretend that it did not happen. The mainstream feminist leadership are apologists for the rich, white elite (the Democrats) who enabled the Republicans to launch these latest assaults on our rights, and they will do it again. With Bush in office, NOW has become bold. They have come out against the war and called for "an end to U.S. foreign policy in the Middle East that exacerbates the plight of women and children in these countries, including U.S. military aggression". Great, but not a word from them about the bombings of or sanctions on Iraq under Clinton. Their current condemnation of U.S. foreign policy is built on a house of sand that will quickly crumble if John Kerry wins.

If the definition of feminism is the end to sexism, then frankly, this mode of thinking is anti-feminist. If I divorce a man because he was taking my money and denying me my basic rights, I cannot see any of these women telling me to marry one of his brothers; yet after eight years of Clinton, that is what the mainstream feminist movement wanted us to do in 2000, and they wanted us to do it again in 2004.

But because of a lack of faith in those who would most benefit from direct involvement, lobbying and voting have taken the place of grassroots political activity. In every election year, there is activity, but its aim is to rally women to the ballot box. The very demographic that WVWV sought to reach is the one that is most receptive to progressive ideas and can jump start a new and true womens' movement, but the movement needs to be democratic, and not top down with a petrified leadership. It also needs to extend far beyond electoral politics.

The march was important, and the mainstream feminist leadership should be praised for calling it. But it would be an insult to the women most affected by the abuse of the Republicans and the neglect of the Democrats to use the energy from this mobilization merely to get out the vote for Kerry and abandon activism after Election Day. No matter the outcome of any particular election, we must build a strong women's movement that will fight relentlessly for what we have lost and dare to envision equality for all.

Chapter 6

"By a brisk accounting of 1993 to 2000, the black stripe of the Rainbow got the Crime Bill, women got 'welfare reform', labor got NAFTA, gays and lesbians got the Defense of Marriage Act. Even with a Democratic Congress in the early years, the peace crowd got no cuts in the military; unions got no help on the right to organize; advocates of DC statehood got nothing (though statehood would virtually guarantee two more Democratic Senate seats and more representation in the House); the single-payer crowd got worse than nothing. Between Clinton's inaugural and the day he left office, 700,000 more persons were incarcerated, mostly minorities; today one in eight black men is barred from voting because of prison, probation or parole."

JoAnn Wypijewski
The Instructive History of Jackson's Rainbow

The Instructive History
of Jackson's Rainbow

ARLY DECEMBER 2003, WHEN THE SMART MONEY WAS
on Howard Dean for the Democratic nomination, when
long-shot bettors were talking about Al Sharpton pulling
a surprise in the South Carolina primary, when nobody but John
Kerry and the Democratic leadership believed the now-pre-
sumptive nominee was "electable", Jesse Jackson was working
the South as if a campaign depended on it.

At South Carolina State, the historically black college where
Strom Thurmond's daughter had studied, little children with
American flags and grown-ups in their Sunday clothes were
waiting on him, while the pep band played and a clutch of
sharply dressed aides talked into their cell phones. Jackson was
late, traveling from a rally in Goose Creek, where police had
raided a high school, forcing 107 kids to their knees, guns to
their head, in a search for drugs that turned up nothing.
Although blacks make up less than a quarter of the student
body, Jackson told the audience after finally bounding onstage,
they accounted for two-thirds of those terrorized in the raid.
Although blacks make up 30 percent of South Carolina's population, they account for 70 percent of its prisoners. The state
spends more on prisons than on all its colleges combined; its
prisoners build auto transmissions while real-paying jobs drain
away.

Twenty years after his first run for the Democratic nomination, Jackson was in his natal state speaking truths on the rigged
rules of race and class that the actual candidates couldn't or
wouldn't, while stressing the imperative of an engaged citizenry
as he had back in the day. "Keep hope alive!" he urged yet again,
and amid an exuberance of cheers there was something in the

sullen silence of a row of teenagers that told the difference between the then and now. Jackson mightn't have noticed. In a flash he was off – to a school, to a preachers' lunch, cell phones a'ringing in the borrowed funeral director's limo, on to Raleigh and thence to Birmingham, "mobilizing the masses," as he put it.

Nobody else was going to do it. For all the candidates' talk about grassroots power, nobody even tried. There are plenty of explanations: the hurry-up primary schedule, the Dean campaign's failure to translate its ground-up fundraising strategy into a similarly oriented investment strategy for indigenous organization; the flimflam of the Sharpton campaign (or "scampaign," as one black South Carolina woman dubbed it) fueled by white Republican dirty-trickster Roger Stone; the relative poverty of the Kucinich camp and its tactical decision to bypass the South, hence African-Americans; the laurel of inevitability conferred upon Kerry after Iowa, even by voters who claimed to dislike him. But the political culture that ordered those choices owes to something older, deeper: to 1984, when Jackson launched a grassroots campaign the likes of which the country had never seen; and to the two roads that diverged out of the ultimate wreckage of that year's general election. One was marked "Rainbow Coalition," the other "The Backlash." The former would launch another presidential campaign in 1988, the most formidable internal party challenge in modern times, and the standard-setter for other grassroots electoral campaigns; the latter would constitute itself as the Democratic Leadership Council, a different kind of internal challenge, one by its own reckoning hostile to the grassroots (it favored the term "special interests") and determined to make the party safe, or safer, for white men.

We live with the legacy of both those efforts, and in a sense both coil back to Jackson. In the American dialectic of race, power and politics, the "legacy" of a black-led, left-leaning, populist challenge would never be a simple thing; if the side of the people was emboldened, so were the tribunes of what Jackson once called "the cash system dominated by white men". If Jackson projected a vision and provided an example of a new kind of movement engagement in electoral politics, the failure to motor that forward must not be his alone. The vital questions on this anniversary, therefore, cannot be neatly contained within the parenthesis of Jackson's personal leaps and limitations. How did progressive forces discharge their responsibilities? How did the Democratic Party respond to the invitation of history? What was gained, and what remains lacking?

Those who did not live in 1984 and 1988 cannot know how sweet a national electoral campaign season can be. Not sweet in the ordinary sense, for there was abundant ugliness – politics is an ugly game – but in that sense where ossification gives way to possibility, where something new appears on the scene that seems to have rearranged the pieces on the playing table, jostled standard assumptions, presented a clear choice. It was Reagan time, and as people suffered, the Democratic Party was in retreat or accommodation. Jackson says now that he never had a mind to run for president, but then the party tops did something that had to be answered. Harold Washington was running for mayor of Chicago in 1983, and "in the middle of his campaign we heard on TV that Ted Kennedy was coming in to support Jane Byrne, and Mondale was coming in to support Daley. We thought, This couldn't be true. These are our guys; we've been with them all along. And we called and sure enough they were coming. So we got together a petition with about a hundred black leaders saying, Please don't come. Please respect our alliance. We could win this election, and it would be, really, a national election – this was Chicago. And they came anyway."

Washington won anyway, powered to victory on what the party leadership couldn't appreciate or failed to notice. For at least ten years a black base had been deepening in Chicago, due in no small measure to Jackson's voter registration efforts and to a methodical training program of Operation PUSH that in the early 1970s taught community people the A to Z of electoral organizing – "the best thing I've ever seen in terms of grassroots politics," according to Frank Watkins, who joined PUSH in 1971 as its "suburban coordinator," organizing white people, and who would later be communications director for the Jackson campaigns.

Meanwhile in Boston, Mel King had put together a multiracial, multiclass coalition – what he was first to call a Rainbow Coalition – in a run for mayor in 1979 and 1983. Nationally, black leftists, frustrated by the prospects for independent politics in the two-party lockbox, were looking for options. And within the black mainstream, people had begun meeting to discuss a response to Reaganism. There too, according to Ron Walters, a political scientist who would coordinate policy briefings for Jackson, the betrayals or indifference of "our guys" in the party featured prominently, and by 1983 the question of What should we demand of them? amped up into Why not go after them? The only remaining matter was Who should run?

That last group "wanted very much not to anoint Jesse Jackson," Walters recalls, and indeed Jackson ran in 1984 without the support, and in many cases with the hostility, of most of the black establishment. (In Montgomery, as recounted by Gwendolyn Patton in a scathing 1984 analysis in *The Journal of Intergroup Relations*, black politicians collaborated with the white media to attack Jackson and his supporters, and even worked the polls against him, offering "unsolicited voter's assistance," that is, infringing on voters' rights.) But Jackson was the candidate of opportunity, and in any case no one else had the moxie to try. Plus Jackson knew the terrain.

"The guy had basically spent the twenty years before that campaigning," said Steve Cobble, who started working with Jackson in 1987 and most recently managed the Kucinich campaign. "No one thought of it as that, but the point is he wasn't going to be showing up the first time as a candidate. That was one of Al's problems this year. It was one of Dennis's problems. You went to these places and even if people liked you, they liked you on paper; they didn't know you. Jackson they knew already. In every state of the country he'd visited, he had people that would offer their church or do some volunteer work or call their network to bring people out." And if he couldn't get there, he knew the black media, he knew the dj's in cities large and small, according to Eric Easter, who would deal with the press during the campaigns. By the time he was running, Jackson would spend every morning doing radio interviews, call-in shows, using free media in a way that only the right wing does now.

More directly, since 1982 Jackson had been on a voter registration crusade throughout the South, which by 1984 would contribute to a 30 percent increase in black registration in the region. In 1980 he'd been on the primary campaign trail, leading marches and rallies on issues he'd hoped Jimmy Carter or Ted Kennedy would take up. He called it a Third Force Strategy. "We were in Ames, Iowa, before the caucus a week after Kennedy was there," says Watkins, now communications director for Congressman Jesse Jackson Jr. "Seven hundred fifty people had come out for Kennedy; 1,000 came for Jackson, and people couldn't get into the place. But we were ignored by the press, ignored by the candidates. I'd actually tried to get Reverend to run in 1979, but he wouldn't do it. Now I told him, 'We're doing what we're supposed to do on the issues, but unless you're a candidate no one will pay attention.'"

And so he ran. "I ran then to challenge our progressive white allies to accept our issues and our pain, not just our votes," Jackson said recently. "We're still convinced, and still trying to convince the party, that expanding the pool of voters is key to winning – but also dealing with the issues that matter to them. Many people want their votes but don't want their issues.

Conservatives try to oppress them; progressives want to wave at 'em but not get involved in the grease and the blood and the grit of dealing with their issues, because their issues create a weighty matter of substance."

Looking back, people who were involved with the campaigns say it was the amplification of issues, many formerly anathema, and the concomitant bolstering of ground forces driving those issues, that are Jackson's profoundest achievements. Walters coordinated twenty-three issue desks in the 1984 campaign, on everything from agricultural policy to nuclear policy. "It was like a school right in the middle of the campaign headquarters," he says. "No one else at that level of national politics was talking about environmental racism, 'no first use' of nuclear weapons (Reagan was talking about 'first strike'); antiapartheid (remember, the ANC was considered a terrorist organization and South Africa a friend); the Arab-Israeli situation." No other Democratic candidate was challenging Reagan's proxy-by-terror in Central America and Africa. None was proposing to cut the military budget and base economic policy on major investment, a program Bill Clinton would run on in 1992 (though abandon forthwith). None at that time regarded gays and lesbians as an intrinsic part of a progressive base, their rights inherent in a larger moral claim and not simply something to be pandered to. None twinned race and class so naturally in an analysis with a global and domestic perspective. None had ever been black.

"Without Jesse, I don't think the antiapartheid movement would have occurred with the strength or vigor that it had here," the historian Manning Marable observed. "The relationships that were forged – Mary Frances Berry, Walter Fauntroy, Randall Robinson, all of them were deeply affected by Jesse's mobilization. Someone could do an analysis of the legacy of the Rainbow called the Class of 1984. Who were the women and men – not just black or Latino, but lesbian and gay, American Indian, white ethnic, the environmentalists who finally acquired a language to appeal to blacks and Latinos, those we now call the anti-prison industrial complex folk, all of those whose action really was unpacked through this Rainbow motion?" A full accounting, according to Eric Easter, who consulted with Dean's campaign this year, can probably never be done. Too many thousands were involved; too many millions potentially came to consciousness. "I think the legacy is in everyone who took what they learned and ran with it" – from Paul Wellstone, whose 1990 senatorial campaign came out of the Rainbow, to the person running the neighborhood organization, to gay activists who created consciously multiracial projects, to the people in Alabama who regained their taste for collective action and planted a garden of organizations.

Certainly, though, says Ron Daniels, who was organizing the Rainbow Coalition in 1987, became deputy campaign manager in 1988 and now directs the Center for Constitutional Rights, "in terms of synthesizing a reformist and radical message, and linking vision to policy to action, especially on apartheid, on the Middle East, those were tremendous contributions, and pretty heavy stuff."

"Madeleine Albright told me at the 1984 convention, 'If you even raise this issue [the question of Palestine], you'll destroy this party," says Jim Zogby, who went from the Arab-American Anti-Discrimination Committee to become deputy campaign manager for fundraising in 1983, a vice president of the Rainbow Coalition and chief campaign fundraiser in 1988. "The debate then was 'Could you even talk to Palestinians?'" – what Jackson describes as "a no-talk policy". "In the middle of all that, for Jackson to say 'Our time, your time, has come' was empowering. It said Arab-Americans were a legitimate political community that had concerns that were not taboo. But those were difficult years. After the convention, Walter Mondale sent back the money Arab-American businessmen contributed to his campaign. When it was found that Gary Hart had taken a loan from an Arab-American bank, he gave it back. After the election the political director of the DNC told me, 'We can't deal with you because if we do another group will be angry with us.' I said that's not only insulting to us, it's anti-Semitic. Jackson urged us, 'Don't give up; the threat you pose is to stick around and fight'. In 1988, I led the platform fight for a plank on mutual recognition and territorial compromise. We had a debate but no vote. We made a dent, but what it took to get there, and this was unprecedented in US history, was huge."

"One of the things that I loved about Jackson, and still do," said Bill Fletcher, now head of TransAfrica Forum and at the time involved in labor efforts in the Rainbow, "is that Jackson refused to be pigeonholed as being a person to speak only on issues of race. In that sense he represented the best in real black political leadership, because it wasn't simply ethnic leadership; it was a leader speaking on all the issues of the day from the perspective of being an African-American, so that that African-Americanness infused his viewpoints. What I have found in most white institutions is a failure to accept that and respect that in people of color. It's a known experience in the labor movement and in many progressive organizations, and I think it was one of the things that was infuriating to much of the Democratic Party officialdom about Jackson."

Including, stresses Gwen Patton, plantation-mentality black officialdom. Despite the cap-L leaders' antipathy, Jackson won a majority of the black vote in Alabama in 1984, as he did nationwide. As she wrote at the time: "Jackson restored human dignity – the essence of freedom which had been sapped by Black politicians in the wake of the people's victory to wrest their citizenship rights from the segregationists. Jackson's candidacy proved that leaders do not stoop to be surrogates for the masses. True leaders are advocates – are waves, as Shirley Chisholm so eloquently says, pushed ahead by the Movement ship steered by the masses." In 1988 Jackson won the Alabama primary outright;

this time black officials were on board ship, and grasping at the controls. Overall, he'd placed third in 1984, with 3.5 million votes, and the pundits who'd said he would be the party's ruin watched as Walter Mondale, heedless of Rainbow constituents and their issues, crashed in defeat. In 1988, Jackson placed second, winning over 7 million votes, more than Mondale had racked up for the nomination in 1984; and 1,218.5 convention delegates, more than any runner-up in history. Again the pundits, here in *The New Republic*, warned of "certain and apocalyptic defeat" if Jackson were given a spot on the Democratic ticket. He wasn't, and Michael Dukakis, as heedless as Mondale and hitched to Lloyd Bentsen, a DLC Democrat, suffered his own private apocalypse.

Jackson likes to tell a story from 1989, about a visit he made to Camp Solidarity in southern Virginia, where the Pittston miners were in the midst of one of the more historic strikes of the 1980s. They were large men for the most part, white for the most part, partial to camouflage, about 10,000 of them. Jackson thought they looked pretty fierce. Rich Trumka, then president of the United Mine Workers, said to them, "Y'awl probably wondering why Jesse Jackson is here. Last year we were told to be scared of him. And this year the folks we gave our money to are nowhere to be seen. So I want you to ask yourselves, 'Which would you rather have, a black friend or a white enemy?'"

It was a question that other Southern white trade unionists had used during the campaign with their memberships, many of them "Reagan Democrats". As elsewhere, the miners answered by listening to Jackson, then gave an enthusiastic response. Jackson always maintained that a progressive candidate could reach such Democrats with straight talk, empathy, class-angled economics and an appeal to common human values – what veteran activist Anne Braden, who'd organized Rainbow rallies in Appalachia that drew thousands of poor white nonvoters or registered Republicans, called "appealing to the best instincts of

Southern whites as opposed to the worst, which is what Bill Clinton played to."

The Pittston story provokes a question, so many years later. After all the energy, vision, galvanizing presence and new voters Jackson brought to the scene, can it be said that the party and established progressive institutions answered in the same way as the plain people? Or did they, perhaps, prefer the white enemy to the black friend?

In reviewing what happened with Rainbow politics after 1988, it's common to focus on Jackson. Certainly, he had sharp critics on the left long before he ran, people who called him, variously, an opportunist, a showboat, a capitalist roader, a man too concerned with mainstream validation, with getting "in," and not enough with the theory and practice of organization. Speaking with Rainbow warriors who had no such misgivings earlier, or shelved them to "follow where the movement was going," is to confront a persistent, deep disappointment that in the spring of 1989 Jackson decided against institutionalizing the Rainbow as a mass-based, democratic, independent membership organization that could pursue the inside-outside strategy he'd articulated vis-à-vis the Democrats and build strength locally and nationally to leverage power for progressive aims. Instead, as Ron Daniels, who'd drawn up various plans for that kind of organization, put it, Jackson opted for "a light and lean operation." It was, Daniels says, "a lost opportunity." Fletcher captures the general tenor of disappointment: "Jackson inspired a level of activity in electoral politics that I've never seen. He encouraged people who were cynical to get involved. The Rainbow pumped people up, and then it deflated them. And the problem is that it then becomes very difficult to reinflate. I think that he overestimated his own strength in the Democratic Party and was seduced by those, particularly in the black political establishment, that suddenly fawned all over him. But what he'd created, rather than a permanent kind of Jackson wing of the party, was a very broad insurgency within and outside the party. And so, ironically, in demobilizing the Rainbow, he also committed a coup against himself."

It would take more than an article to unravel all the hurts and hopes, the calculations and miscalculations. And because that other organization – imagined as a left variant on the Christian Coalition – never materialized, the might-have-beens are frozen in the amber of conjecture. Jackson himself says, "I like that idea. It's a good idea. But it would've required infrastructure and resources and discipline. You can't just wish something like that into working." Privately, one of his close campaign associates said, "I think Jackson didn't want to have to referee between different parts of his coalition. By 1988 the tensions were already clear. The activists were getting supplanted by the elected officials; the Congress people were telling the lefty radicals to tone it down. The sectarians in various places were trying to take it over internally, and you know the left has never solved that question. We had the most diverse, most little-d democratic, most American delegation anybody's ever sent to a convention in 1988. But if we had just had grassroots little-d democratic votes everywhere, we'd have had a delegation made up almost entirely of black ministers because in any given city they could outvote certainly the gay and lesbian representative, certainly the white Central America activists, the Asian-Americans. Some state coordinators are still catching hell for the choices they made to get the delegation that we had. So I think Jackson saw this endless series of confrontations in a lose-lose situation where he'd get to divide his troops." No doubt, says Anne Braden, "when he started coming to Rainbow meetings after the campaign he probably thought he had a tiger by the tail, and maybe he felt he couldn't control it. But on the Rainbow board, people felt we were doing fine. He needed to trust the people more who really wanted to make it work." Privately others say Jackson is simply incapable of engaging in the kind of dialogue and delegation of authority that sustaining that type of organization would have required.

But if that debate is full of unknowns, plenty of knowns can still prick the conscience. In 1984, as Andrew Kopkind and Alexander Cockburn wrote in *The Nation*, Jackson and the Rainbow represented the historical base and radical message for which the left had been yearning in an electoral wilderness. Yet labor, NOW, black and Hispanic leaders, Democratic Socialists, organized gays and lesbians, whites mustered in various other likely constituencies went their own way or, worse, into the arms of Mondale, who, like John Kerry today, had accepted the essential premises of the Republican program, except tax cuts, and quarreled merely with the execution. Between 1984 and 1988, as Steve Cobble notes, "no one of any prominence among white progressives came to Jackson and said 'We want you to run'; none of the magazines, none of the organizations, only a couple of labor unions (AFGE, the Machinists, 1199). In 1988 AFSCME did a split with him and Dukakis in different cities. The only large organization that wasn't black that backed him was ACORN. The first publication to endorse was the *Texas Observer*, in early March. *The Nation* didn't until April, which was pretty dang late. After 1988 Jackson clearly now is the frontrunner for the nomination. Did the unions get together and say, 'Jesse, let's go, let's start right now for 1992'? Did any of the liberal organizations? No. NOW had its convention in '89 and announced it was putting together a commission to study a third party. Jackson's the front-runner for the major party nomination, and as soon as he gets that position suddenly they're thinking about organizing a third party!"

"Front-runner" talk always disconcerts leftists who supported the Jackson campaigns for their presumed organizational, more than electoral, potential. And yet in one sense it is clarifying. Whatever else he could or couldn't do, Jackson was a proven, powerful candidate. His grassroots forays were credited with helping the Democrats win back the Senate in 1986 and propelling a host of candidates into office at the local, state and national level. By the calculus through which liberal institutions ordinarily come to support Democrats, the nod to Jackson should have been uncontroversial. A labor official, asked why, especially after Dukakis's drubbing, unions would not have seen where their own future best interests lay, said, "That's not the way those people do business; they don't do the outreach." But there was nothing business-as-usual about Jackson, who'd walked picket lines for decades. Frank Watkins was more direct: "The reason labor didn't do that is they're racist. The reason civil rights organizations didn't is they're jealous. The reason the women didn't is they're suspicious."

Someone else, of course, was doing outreach in the spring of '89. Al From, intellectual architect of the Democratic Leadership Council, paid a visit that season to Governor Bill Clinton in Little Rock, suggesting that the DLC could be the vehicle for his ambitions and laying the ground for the policy, personnel and financial relationships that would become the infrastructure of Clinton's 1992 campaign. Unlike the progressive forces, the backlash Democrats recognized the utility of a charismatic candidate upon which to pin their electoral hopes, and of starting early. For 1984 they'd won rules changes in the party, introducing the concept of "superdelegates" to shift power at the conventions from party activists to elected officials. Jackson managed to negotiate limits on those delegates at the 1984 convention. The next year the DLC formally constituted itself. For 1988 it advocated one big Southern primary, Super Tuesday, which it expected, out of arrogance or inattention, would secure the nomination for a Southern white conservative. Jackson swept Super Tuesday, besting the DLC's favorite son, Al Gore. When Jackson then took 54 percent of the vote in Michigan, what appeared in tantalizing prospect was a new party paradigm – neither the New Deal alliance of Northern liberals, blue collars and Jim Crow, nor post-McGovern liberalism with its smorgas-bord of interests and its white elite firmly in charge of portion-control. Party liberals had a choice; they chose reaction.

As outlined in Kenneth Baer's sympathetic book, *Reinventing Democrats*, From and Co. were straightforward about their vision of rolling back the party to its pre-civil rights past, where the issues of "special interests" would be submerged to the goal of winning, and winning would mean reinstituting what Congressman Jesse Jackson Jr. calls the "Democratic Legacy of the Confederacy." In the run-up to the 1992 race, Clinton's people, as recounted in Marshall Frady's book *Jesse*, would confer with the old captains of the Mondale campaign asking, "Why did you guys give so much to Jackson? You shouldn't've got pushed around like that." In the campaign, Clinton would push back at Jackson, at labor. The iconic image of 1992 would be Clinton and Senator Sam Nunn posing at Stone Mountain, Georgia, the graven images of the generals of the Confederacy looming in the background, and in the middle distance, a chain gang of black prisoners.

"The error," says Kevin Gray, who coordinated Jackson's winning campaign in South Carolina in 1988 and organized for the 1984 win as well, "was in assuming we ever left the Age of Reagan. We, and by that I mean the so-called progressive community, never carried the critique to the Age of Clinton. Where Jesse dropped the ball is he became a Democrat. Instead of a small-d democrat, he became a big-D Democrat – except with an asterisk."

Asterisk?

"You know the line, 'World champions and you MVP, you a nigger,/Four degrees and a PhD, still a nigger.' And that's exactly how I think the Democratic Party sees Jesse. Now, I have dis-agreements with the brother – I think he squandered his lever-age, which was our leverage, because the beauty of Jesse running was the threat that we all might one day walk, or even the threat to disrupt things, and for African-Americans in this political system, hell, that's the only power we got. That and moral authority, especially as relates to a Democratic Party that styles itself as having the interests of black folk at heart. Are they living up to it? Hell no. But, now, everybody else got to look in that mirror too. What did the Rainbow stripes get from Bill Clinton? And where was everybody else, where were progressive forces on that?"

By a brisk accounting of 1993 to 2000, the black stripe of the Rainbow got the Crime Bill, women got "welfare reform," labor got NAFTA, gays and lesbians got Defense of Marriage Act. Even with a Democratic Congress in the early years, the peace crowd got no cuts in the military; unions got no help on the right to organize; advocates of DC statehood got nothing (though statehood would virtually guarantee two more Democratic Senate seats and more representation in the House); the single-payer crowd got worse than nothing. On affirmative action, Jackson had to threaten Clinton privately with an independent run in 1996 before the president declared the weaselish "mend it, don't end it." Manning Marable points out that between Clinton's inaugural and the day he left office, 700,000 more persons were incarcerated, mostly minorities; today one in eight black men is barred from voting because of prison, probation or parole. "Talk about amputating your base," says Marable. Ideologically, of course, it was not Clinton's base, the DLC base, that was attacked, amputated. It was Jackson's base, the rainbow base. Divided, we fell.

The day that Ronald Reagan died, Jackson was preparing to barnstorm through Appalachia. There was a curious historical symmetry about it. Twenty years ago, as Reagan lashed out at "welfare queens" and projected a fantasyland America from his White House sinecure, Jackson was in those same hills and hollows, pressing against the flesh and suffered facts of the real thing – striving, as he put it, "to deracialize the debate about poverty" and, as a black candidate in white territory, to test the proposition that "the people are beyond where our political fears are." It was the children of those hills about whom Reagan had said, Let them eat ketchup! and whom America today has sent to kill and die in Iraq. "Why are we going to Appalachia?" Jackson said. "Because that's where our soul is." Our shame, too, he might have added; along with the Black Belt South, it is the region with the most unemployment, the poorest people, the sickest people, the most persistent underdevelopment, whichever party holds power and however officially prosperous the time. Urging "Reinvest in America" and amplifying the right to vote, to learn, to be cared for against sickness and need, to organize a union, the tour, through old mining and steel counties of Pennsylvania, West Virginia and Ohio, was being sponsored by Rainbow/PUSH and a long list of unions that had never put their names to a Rainbow campaign. For Jackson it was Third Force all over again, including the blackout from a press gorging on the myth of Reagan, man of the people. Unmentioned in the obsequies over the Reagan legacy, including what George Stephanopoulos noted as Clinton's work to "complete Reagan's agenda," were the resistance efforts - around AIDS, around apartheid and Central America, around the Jackson campaigns - that would set the political vectors for people on the left just coming to consciousness in the 1980s and for their little brothers and sisters.

"I do not approach America cynically," Jackson said shortly before leaving for Appalachia, "because I did not know a day where we did not have to struggle. This year people ask about anniversaries - fifty years since Brown, forty years since the Civil Rights Act - and say 'What happened in fifty years?' It's a good question, but what about what happened before fifty years? For 335 years race supremacy was the law of the land. Then the law changed but the culture didn't change. The idea of a nonracist society, legally, is just fifty years old. The idea of an open, inclusive democracy is just thirty-seven years old. When we ran, the Voting Rights Act was just nineteen years old. So it's still early in the morning. And it's a bit different between African-Americans and our white progressive allies. For us, liberals and conservatives are often two sides of the same coin. No liberal ever had to fight to use a toilet. No liberal ever had to fight for the right to vote, fight to stay in a hotel, fight to buy ice cream at a Howard Johnson's with money. No liberal is scared today because there are so many ways the constituency can be killed. And there's a culture that goes with that. So you're always fighting two battles. You're fighting the culture in your own huddle, your own party, as you're fighting the other side. You're pushing political ideas and cultural transformation at the same time. What was gratifying about the campaigns was moving that process, and that process is irreversible."

Downstairs from where we were talking, a conference of Democratic progressives was underway. At first glance a blinding sea of white, it was a little different among the younger cohort, where Rainbowism in practice seemed to have more root. There, they were talking about technology but also shoe-leather "beauty parlor/barbershop" organizing; about voter registration but also something beyond "which white man to vote for"; about using electoral politics as a bridge to another kind of politics because "our issues don't go away after the election"; about remembering that "the people need hope" but also regarding the Democratic Party without illusion. The name Kerry never came up. The issues they identified as theirs fell within what, upstairs, Jackson had called "the trilogy of racism, exploitative capitalism and militarism," what Martin Luther King had been the first to call "the triple evils that are interrelated." They were in their 20s and 30s, and in their discussion there was the resonance of something I'd heard from Jack O'Dell, an old soldier of the left, who'd worked with Dr. King, worked with Jackson, shaping the international agenda. "There are moments," he'd said, "and we have to take from those moments all that is positive, because that's our inheritance. Because of Jesse Jackson's campaigns, we know how to build a grassroots campaign. Without them, we might have the analysis but not the experience to do what we need to do. We must still ask ourselves how we can reinvigorate electoral democracy. We can't drop out, as if what we don't like about electoral politics will go away because we abstain. Movements are directed toward political power, and wherever we can get a piece of it, we have to try to get it and hold onto it. Now, we know what Bush is. If we are victorious in defeating Bush, then our assignment is to make what we can of Kerry. And our job begins the next day."

Chapter 7

"No other president in United States history has managed to get so much black support for giving so little. But what makes Clinton's race act so successful is that black America never asked him to do much to begin with."

Kevin Alexander Gray
Clinton and Black Americans

Kevin Alexander Gray

Clinton and Black Americans

"[Clinton] has always wanted our love and wanted to share his love with us.... It is not about the skin. It is about the spirit and the soul of this soul brother."
– Former Transportation Secretary Rodney Slater

I WAS MILDLY AMUSED, A BIT DISGUSTED BUT NOT SURPRISED, when former President Bill Clinton was named to the Arkansas Black Hall of Fame. Unfortunately, there is no shortage of gullibility when it comes to the relationship between blacks and the man from Hope. Towards the end of his term, he was viewed favorably by a staggering 83 percent of African Americans. Now Clinton has been named honorary chairman of the planned $37 million national Museum of African American History expected to open in Charleston in 2007.

Besides just having a big name draw to raise money, it should be obvious what's going on. Clinton is reworking his image by creating a phony civil rights legacy. Forced to resign because of Watergate, Richard Nixon attempted to reshape his image into that of a foreign policy expert before his death. Jimmy Carter left office a failure with hostages in Iran and an economy in crisis. He was still able to remake himself into a statesman and international peace advocate. Should Clinton get his way, memories of his real race record will fade as he transmogrifies himself into a racial healer. And he is getting plenty of help, as always, from black people.

Charles King, the hall of fame's executive director, said the former president deserved induction "to show him our appreciation not only for what he did as president but for his lifelong association with us. He came to us. We were responsible for him being governor, and president. He held on to that. And we held on to that."

Clinton is now the only white person among the hall's 62 members, who include poet Maya Angelou, John Johnson, founder of *Jet* and *Ebony* magazines, and former Clinton administration Surgeon General Joycelyn Elders. Remember Elders? Clinton fired her because she said it wasn't a bad idea to talk about masturbation in sex education classes.

The evening of the induction Clinton shared the dais with soul-turned-gospel singer/preacher Al Green. The two have so much in common that it's a wonder Clinton hasn't had a pot of hot grits flung at him. Point being – their commonalty has more to do with them being doggish, busted males than some twisted sense of racial or cultural empathy.

Since leaving office, Clinton has been working his "ghetto pass" overtime. When complaints arose about the cost of his office space in Midtown Manhattan, what did he do? He moved to 125th Street in Harlem, historically the intellectual capital of black America. The community that nurtured Malcolm X, Langston Hughes, Claude McKay, Jessie Fauset, W.E.B. Du Bois, Zora Neale Hurston, Adam Powell and a host of others ate it up. Harlem was Clinton's second choice and for that he got a hero's welcome.

At present, the only national political figure the Democratic Party has – black or white – that blacks identify with is Clinton. In 1998 the party's get-out-the-black-vote effort consisted of mailing out postcards with Clinton posing beside black families. In the 2002 elections black households once again got their postcards with Clinton's picture followed up by an automated phone message from their good buddy Bill.

No other president in United States history has managed to get so much black support for giving so little. But what makes Clinton's race act so successful is that black America never asked him to do much to begin with. In the 1980s, Clinton was the first white candidate for governor to reach out to Arkansas's black voters, to eat on their porches, pray in their churches, invite them into the governor's office. For 12 years before Clinton, Ronald Reagan and George Bush insulted and ignored black people. Consequently, when Clinton wooed African Americans, most were just happy someone was finally paying attention. To some degree, black support of Clinton is also acknowledgement of the black community's need for white acceptance.

Some argue that Clinton deserves support because his economic policies were a boon for African Americans. During his administration median income reached an all-time high, and poverty among blacks dipped thanks in large part to his increases in the minimum wage and the Earned Income Tax Credit. But on the other side of the economic coin the black-white wealth disparity remained fixed and the gap between the rich and poor expanded under his administration.

Others point to the record number of African Americans in the Clinton cabinet and the picture of racial diversity it projected. At times Clinton talked the social justice talk, lavishly invoking the name of Martin Luther King. While touring Africa he even gave a half-hearted apology for America's part in European colonization and enslavement. A black man, Vernon Jordan, was his best friend. A black woman, Betty Currie, was his personal secretary. It's debatable whether the blacks around Clinton had any real power, but real or not, his mostly symbolic gestures were much more than black people had ever seen from a white person in power. And those gestures have carried Clinton a long way.

The joke that refuses to go away has Clinton as America's first black president – a sentiment enthusiastically affirmed by black celebrities, elites and quasi-intellectuals. In his bit, comedian Chris Rock used Clinton's "persecution over a $300 haircut" to support the claim. Former Southern Christian Leadership Conference head Joseph Lowery said that blacks like Clinton because "he plays the saxophone." Harvard professor Alvin Poussaint joked, Clinton "must have black ancestry". Back in 1998 during the height of the Monica Lewinsky scandal, writer Toni Morrison said, "black skin notwithstanding: this is our first black President" citing his dysfunctional upbringing as commonality with black males. But the joke's an insult. The punch line is that Clinton is decadent and promiscuous, got rhythm, got caught and got over — so he's black!

The notion of Clinton as a great friend of the black community or defender of civil rights is just as crazy. Clinton co-opted civil rights themes and figures and distorted their meaning for his political advancement and survival. Whether it's his telling blacks how disappointed "Dr. King would be [in them] if he were alive today", because of black on black crime or his attorney comparing him to Abraham Lincoln during the impeachment hearings, Clinton was an expert at playing the race card. All the while, his policies and attitude on due process, equal protection and equal treatment, or civil rights (rights guaranteed to all), were horrible. A couple of examples of his racial hypocrisy come to mind. One was his initiative requiring citizens, mostly black, in public housing to surrender their Fourth Amendment or privacy rights. Another was the "one strike and you're out" policy under which public housing residents convicted of a crime, along with anyone who lives with them, are evicted without consideration of their due process rights. But while the Rehnquest Court upheld these assaults on the rights of the poor, Jeb Bush (via his daughter Nicole) and Clinton (still on the public dole) all remain exempt from the laws they promote.

Southern politician Clinton has always played the race-crime game to perfection. In his first presidential race Governor Clinton ran for office supporting the death penalty at a time when the country was split almost down the middle on the issue. Then for good measure, he rushed back to Arkansas to oversee the execution of convicted killer Ricky Ray Rector, a brain-damaged black man. For years after his first election, I kept a picture of Clinton and Georgia Senator Sam Nunn posing in front of a phalanx of black inmates in white prison suits taken at Stone Mountain, Georgia. Historians generally give Pulaski, Tennessee, the dubious honor as the birthplace of the Ku Klux Klan. But Stone Mountain is hailed as the Klan's second home. The picture appeared in newspapers all across the south the day of the southern primaries in 1992. That picture is what Clinton has always represented to me.

So, the fact that Clinton left behind a larger – mostly black – prison population than when he took office should come as no surprise. Black incarceration rates during the Clinton years surpassed Ronald Reagan's eight years. The incarceration rates for blacks increased from around 3,000 per 100,000 to 3,620 per 100,000 people during his administration. That he did nothing about mandatory minimum sentences was no surprise. That he did nothing to change the sentencing disparity between crack and powder cocaine that disproportionately affects African Americans was no surprise. That he successfully stumped for "three strikes and you're out" in the crime bill, for restrictions on the right of habeas corpus and expansion of the federal death penalty was no surprise. When he came into office one in four black men were in the toils of the criminal justice system in some way; when he left it was one in three. In many states ex-felons are denied the right to vote, a factor that had a direct impact on the 2000 presidential vote in Florida. Again, no surprise.

Shortly after leaving office, Clinton published a piece, "Erasing America's Color Lines", in the *New York Times*. He wrote that "America was now at a point where we can write a new preamble to the 21st century, in which color differences are not the problem, but the promise, of America." He outlined a path that would allow the Bush administration to reduce systemic racism.

The list included a ban on racial profiling, an examination of mandatory minimum sentencing and a presidential commission on voter reform.

But Clinton's suggestions were another bit of hypocrisy given that he refused to implement them while he had the chance. And his knowledge that George Bush would never take any of his suggestions made the whole exercise just another piece of grotesque symbolism, typical of his relationship with the black community. The commentary was a perfect postscript to Clinton's marriage with black America, a relationship that is characterized by the James Brown song "Talking Loud and Saying Nothing".

On the night Clinton was inducted into the Arkansas hall of fame, Charles King must have lost his memory. He forgot that, as Governor, his guest of honor refused to sign a civil rights bill. In Charleston, the people behind the civil rights museum forgot that Clinton dumped his friend Lani Guinier from consideration for the Justice Department's office of civil rights over her advocacy of cumulative voting – the next frontier for civil rights, which would break down voting by race and party.

Maybe Clinton's name and service on the board in Charleston will help lure the money needed to make the project a reality. Maybe now blacks will get to use him and maybe get something in return for a change. But he shouldn't be allowed simply to fundraise himself into a legacy or assume a legacy he doesn't deserve. A legacy should be more that just showing up. As for being a soul brother? He's got a very, very long way to go.

Chapter 8

"What the Democrats have managed to do on the North Coast is create an old fashioned political machine that creates jobs for people who believe that Democrats are 'progressive'. Maybe they are in some places, but not here. Here, in real life practice, Democrats are Bush Republicans. To use one of their favorite words, Democrats are 'facilitators' of environmental and social destruction."

Bruce Anderson
Notes from the Big Empty

BRUCE ANDERSON
Notes from the Big Empty

DEMOCRATS IN ACTION? HOW ABOUT IN MENDOCINO County, California, a great big rugged rural place with 85,000 people strewn over an area larger than Vermont. The short history of the Democratic Party takeover of Mendocino County goes like this: Beginning in 1967, thousands of hippies drove north on Highway 101 from the Bay Area, headed "back to the land". The land they were going back to was cheap, and got cheaper the farther north their used Volvos carried them. But when the urban refugees, themselves refugees from the suburbs and everything represented by suburbs, got back to the land, there was no hippie way to support themselves other than dope production, and dope's a high stress enterprise given the cops, thieves and the IRS. So a lot of the hippies dusted off their diplomas, cleaned up and drove down out of the hills to get themselves public jobs, which in the perennially tight economy of Mendocino County are the only jobs that pay college people the kind of money college people think they deserve.

The hippies were re-entering the society they'd spent their youths being contemptuous of. And being middle-class and civic-minded, they soon elected other hippies, or hip-symps, to a few low-level offices, then some mid-level offices, until Mendocino County's public jobs were entirely dominated by the love generation.

And public policy in Mendocino County grew crueler by the year, in direct proportion to the re-entry return of the formerly estranged. For $30,000 a year, a flower child would put the figurative, the programmatic boots to anybody a rung down the ladder.

Pay an old hippie with a law degree $140,000 a year with the full fringe package for him and Mrs. Lib and the kids, and he'll kill, which is what Mendocino County's seven liberal judges, all of them Up From Hippie, do five days a week every week in the Mendocino County Courthouse.

"Life without, punk, but I feel your pain".

Congressman Mike Thompson picked up a Purple Heart in Vietnam. He said when he got home a hippie spit on him. Thompson runs unopposed for re-election. The Republicans don't bother putting money into an opponent because they've got Thompson who's just as good.

Thompson presides over an apparatus of career officeholders like himself who replace each other when one of them moves on to another public office.

If no public office is immediately available to a term-limited old boy, the Democrats park him or her on a state board of some kind at a hundred thousand a year for one meeting a week until another old boy leaves another safe seat open.

The electoral base camp for rotating offices consists almost entirely of public employees, whose funding depends on Democrats at the state and federal levels. The edu-bloc votes as one for Democrats, the Democrats send money and promise to send more without raising taxes. People employed at various levels of government – and that's a lot of people in Mendocino County, one third of everyone employed – vote Democratic because the Democrats can be depended on to make more government, especially of the kind that keeps on re-electing them. What the Democrats have managed to do on the North coast is create an old fashioned political machine that creates jobs for people who believe that Democrats are "progressive". Maybe they are in some places, but not here. Here, in real life practice, Democrats are Bush Republicans. To use one of their favorite words, Democrats are "facilitators" of environmental and social destruction.

This is the county whose sheriff and district attorney, libertarian Republicans, ran for office promising to decriminalize marijuana. Which they did, and both were re-elected by even greater margins the second time they ran. They've also passed out more concealed weapons permits than any DA and Sheriff in the state. They're at odds with Democrats and Republicans on most issues, but you won't hear a critical word from either of them ever on the deficiencies of the career officeholders of the Democratic machine.

We have a thriving Green Party that votes for Democrats and steadfastly avoids running candidates for local office. When the rare Green takes on the Democrats, he's either stabbed by Democrats or denounced by Greens for not having been sanctioned by them. When Green guy Dave Severn took on a semipsychotic Democrat for county supervisor, the Mendocino Green Party refused to endorse Severn. When an elected school board trustee and registered Green signed up for the Green congressional primary this year hoping to oppose Congressman Thompson in the general election in November, a recreational candidate who runs for office on one minority party ballot or another every election, just happened to find $500 to register to run against the viable Green in the Green primary. The recreational candidate, who is neither seen nor heard on any issue between elections, beat the legitimate Green in the primary because she's a woman and she has a Mexican-sounding surname. The legit Green would have caused incumbent Thompson some serious anxiety in his re-election race against a token Republican because Thompson, like Gore and Kerry on the national level, inspires either zero enthusiasm or negative enthusiasm of the I'll-vote-for-the-Greens-just-to-screw-things-up-for-the-two-party-dictatorship variety.

Congressman Thompson, Wine Country representative all the way and the industry's main man in Washington, was instrumental in getting the ban on methyl bromide delayed for five more years on behalf of his industry padrones. Thompson, not deigning to take out the necessary permits, bulldozed a parcel of land he owns in nearby Lake County so he could put in his own little vineyard, rightly assuming the authorities would pretend not to know he did it.

The wine people are heavily Democratic because Democrats, they seem to think, have panache; Republicans don't. It is hard to imagine John Ashcroft at a wine tasting, not hard to imagine Bill and Hillary at one, the crazed AG is not a likely white wine and brie guy. But a rhetorically liberal upscale couple would be right at home in a setting of the superficial and the silly.

Pumped down into the soil to depths of 12 feet, methyl bromide sterilizes the earth as grape vine site prep. Immigrant Mexicans, dressed in protective moonsuits, apply the lethal stuff, and often die in industry accidents involving ag or industrial wine chemicals, especially nitrogen, because the wine people, thanks to Democrats, are basically exempt from industrial safety standards.

The wine industry, heavy consumers of pesticides and herbicides, is environmentally devastating and socially indifferent; they clearcut large swaths of land with a thoroughness the most demented logger can only dream of doing, then lay on the chemicals year round. Socially, the industry provides little to no worker housing for the immigrant labor upon which depends. The wine industry, which seldom pays better than minimum wages for seasonal work, rises up as one to crush UFW organizing attempts like so many grapes, and fires any worker who complains without so much as promising anything resembling a fair hearing. Congressman Thompson, a Democrat who's interchangeable with Republicans on most votes, is the wine industry's national go-to guy.

One spring morning back in the 1970s, as a clusters of little hippie kids waited for the big yellow school bus to carry them to classrooms as dull and reactionary as the ones their alienated parents had fled for California's backwoods, a Louisiana-Pacific helicopter, spraying the freshly-logged hills with herbicides to prevent non-commercial re-vegetation, heedlessly sprayed the little Rainbows and Karmas as they waited for their school buses. The hippies mobilized and passed an aerial spray ban. Within months, state Democrats, including those elected from this area, led by Willie Brown, all of their pockets stuffed with corporate ag cash, passed legislation that decreed that individual counties couldn't regulate herbicides and pesticides – only the state could decide on the big ticket stuff like who could poison the kids and who couldn't. You don't like Garlon dropped on your kid? Take it up with Sacramento.

AMONG THE RE-ENTRY HIPPIES WHO DOMINATE MENDOCINO County's public institutions are too many lawyers. Law degreed hippies were quick to note that Mendocino County's far-flung communities were served by one-day-a-week justice courts whose judges were "lay persons", i.e., non-lawyers. Nobody in Mendocino County was unhappy with the lay judges in any organized sense of unhappiness; lay judges were a non-issue. People living in the deep outback liked their judges and their courts the way they were, but the lawyers scented opportunity. The lawyers, especially the under-employed ones barely able to earn enough to support the hepatitis lifestyle they'd moved to the country to pursue, began to say, "The quality of justice is likely to be inferior if the person dispensing it isn't properly trained. We really should have lawyers sitting as judges in these justice courts". The law was changed, and the lay judges, who had dispensed Mendocino County justice for a hundred years, were gone. Trained legal professionals, fresh from the big naked solstice piles up in the hills, took over Mendocino County's justice courts.

There's been a dramatic change in the quality of justice. Not only are more people than ever going to jail, a new lawyer judge fell in love with an armed robber defendant and, time and again, tossed the charges against his boy friend until people said, "Hey! If this guy would rob people over the hill we wouldn't mind you sleeping with him, your honor. But we live here!"

The lawyer judge went, but the judge who replaced him, an exhibitionist, kept flashing his court's female staffers. He finally went off for "counseling", but came back after a few months of working as a judge an hour away; his judicial pals said privately they'd told him to be sure to wear clothes under his robes, and keep his gonads off the scales of justice.

Lay judges made $300 a month for one-day-a-week. The lawyer judges make $140,000 a year plus fringes for themselves and their families. They can work or not work, as they please; they can stay home and draw their base pay or travel around the state at public expense to sit as visiting judges.

We've got more of these $140,000 judges than any population our size in the state. And the justice courts? They're gone, centralized so the judges don't have to travel much. The elevation of hippie judges to superior court status was sold as "reorganization" and "increased efficiency". The Democrat-dominated state legislature sold us that one.

The quality of justice now that long-time pot smokers are presiding? If you can afford a well-connected lawyer you get off; if you can't you go to the state pen, and the people sending you are all NPR listeners, Democrats, liberals, Clintonians.

A 19-year-old kid recently got sent off on, as they say, an L-WOP, life without the possibility of parole. He got a one-day jury trial during which his public defender called no witnesses on his behalf, assigned no investigators to look at the facts of the case, wrapped up by denouncing the kid as a very bad person who'd committed a very bad murder. Her defense? The boy hadn't been properly read his rights. The jury was back within minutes with a unanimous guilty verdict. Even the cops were stomping indignantly around the courthouse at the public defender's grotesquely inept defense.

The L-WOP boy's two accomplices, one of whom did the murder, got 15 and 19 years respectively. Everyone involved in the case's second murder, the judicial murder of this L-WOP kid now buried for life at Soledad, is a registered Democrat. The sentencing judge is an active Democrat whose wife works in the local Democrat Assemblyperson's office.

We even have an "alternate public defender's" office, a jobs program for under-employed but hip-lib lawyers. The way this works, and it works at enormous additional expense to taxpayers, is when one of the regular public defenders claims "a conflict of interest", the "alternate" is summoned. The conflict can be as vague as a remote commercial association from, say, five years ago when the defendant attended the same wedding as one of the attorneys in the public defender's office. The faux scrupulousness is really just a way to spread the legal work around the Democrats who, of course, delude themselves into thinking they're fighters for the underdog.

We also have a family court magistrate; and two court administrators; and privatized court reporters (two of whom are girlfriends of sitting judges), and family court mediators, invariably ex-hippies whose own lives are hopelessly fucked up but drawing nice pay to help other fucked up people with their marital woes, usually making them worse, and we have victim witness coordinators; and a triple-sized probation department; and family court advocates; and on and on – at least a thousand 'helping professionals', and not a Republican in the bunch, and the whole mob of them committed Democrats of the type who write letters to the editor denouncing Ralph Nader.

Mendocino County, having gone big time for Dean, later went big time for Kerry. Our local public radio station, partially funded by WalMart and the local wine industry, both of which are entirely dependent on grotesquely exploited labor, bills itself as "Free Speech Radio, Mendocino County". It's dominated by Democrats, and there are exactly two hours a month of aggressively vetted semi-free speech. Pacifica Network-type Stalinists answer the phones, and if you aren't talking Kucinich or Kerry or Mumia or their local surrogates, you don't get to talk. No dissent is allowed on air. Ever. But the Democrats get all the air time they want, and since there are no Republicans who either tune in or call in during the two whole hours a month any old body can reach right out and audio touch a tax-paid censor, it's all Democrats all the time.

As in the rest of America, the Democrats stay in office here in Ecotopia by routing funding to public employees. School people and public employees vote as a bloc for Democrats because Democrats fund them. Local food banks estimate that a minimum of 20 percent of Mendocino County children under the age of five don't get enough to eat, and many Mendocino County schools fail to meet prevailing educational standards, low as they are. The Mendocino County Jail, because it has had to take over the care and feeding of the ill because Mendocino County's helping professionals, many of them active Democrats, and all of them Democratic voters although occasionally registered Green, aren't equal to the task; the jail is so overcrowded it regularly releases its least violent inmates after they've served a third to half their sentences.

The proprietor of a fancy, ocean view inn is "environmental chair" of California's Democratic Party. During grassroots demonstrations against the possibility that the Pacific off the Mendocino Coast might eventually be drilled for oil, Democrats like Gray Davis, known locally as Eraser Head, showed up in chauffeur-driven gas guzzlers for environmental photo-ops. The inn owner, previously unengaged in the agitation to keep oil rigs out of her viewshed, inserted herself into the turmoil, sedate as it was, and was soon appearing in the *New York Times* as the lady who's saving the sea from Chevron. Her inn became a regular pit stop for bigwig Democrats, and she became the person who kept the derricks off the North coast. The grassroots people, who'd hoped for a permanent ban on offshore drilling, were shoved aside, and the safety of sea creatures has been in the well-oiled, well-funded hands of Democrats ever since.

So have the forests, what's left of them. When the North Coast grassroots drew national attention to the grim fact that outside timber corporations were cashing in Mendocino and Humboldt county trees for short-term profit and long-term environmental and employment devastation, the grassroots turned to their Democratic officeholders for help. The Democrats, always ready to oblige, helped the corporations mop up what was left of both the private and public trees, and then, with public money freed up by Clinton, bought up untouched acres of forest at twice their already inflated value from Charles Hurwitz, a junk bond tycoon based in Texas who does big business deals with Senator Dianne Feinstein's husband.

The Democrats and their local gofers also negotiated a set aside of thousands of acres of land at Big River, just south of tourist ground zero, Mendocino Village. The newest set aside was dedicated to two active Democrats who'd always been among the missing when environmental push had come to environmental shove. It's as if long time environmentalists like Ron Guenther, who literally risked his neck to take on the timber corporations and was the first local person to protest timber harvest plans on their merits, was ignored as Democrats and their officeholders held a self-congratulatory hand-over ceremony at Big River beach.

The *New York Times*-owned Santa Rosa *Press Democrat* serves as major media stenographer for local Democrats. The paper was distraught at Gray Davis's recall as California's governor. "We just can't allow voters to monkeywrench things like this", the paper wailed editorially. "What if the mob goes after Wes or Patti or Mike and the rest of our progressive friends? It's too terrible to contemplate".

The Davis recall lost in Mendocino County. The Democrats managed to convince the minority of eligible voters who bothered with the recall election that Davis was better than the alternative. The alternative was, of course, a lateral move, electorally considered, and here we are again with the Democrats telling us that it's Kerry or another four years of Bush.

In Mendocino County, it's another four years of Thompson as methyl bromide's national advocate, while here with the home folks, Thompson's in-county rep, long ago secretly anointed by the Thompson Democrats to become a supervisor and thus begin her climb upwards to the imported brie, easily defeated an unblessed male Democrat to get the job.

In November, 2004, the Mendocino County Board of Supervisors will consist of five Democrats: a gay woman; a recovering alcoholic; a retired rock and roll musician; a trust fund hippie; and a Bly Guy who changed his name to Wildman: rural multiculturalism, Democrat style.

Chapter 9

"Max Baucus may still be the most corporate-entrenched, conniving Democrat in Washington, and Montana has suffered tremendously as a result. Low employment. A broken public school system. A degraded natural environment. The exponential evaporation of the family farm. Montana's hurting, and the Democrats – most certainly Baucus – don't seem to give a damn."

Josh Frank
The Slick Swindler Senator Max Baucus

JOSH FRANK

The Slick Swindler
Senator Max Baucus

AT THE NAÏVE AGE OF 18, WHILE STILL IN HIGH SCHOOL, I had the pleasure of flying across the country to Washington, D.C., for a weeklong youth workshop on leadership and democracy. I remember the teary excitement I had knowing I was about to meet both of my Montana senators. Back then I was a proud registered Democrat. Having joined the party only two months earlier, I felt the prospect of rubbing shoulders with a veteran of my party was sure to be the highlight of my trip.

The swank décor of the hallways on the Hill mesmerized me as I winded through the legislative chambers. The bright carpet and gorgeous young interns meandering around the foyers made me think that perhaps politics had its subtle rewards. My intrepid journey from wing to wing led me to the bustling office of Montana Senator Max Baucus.

Max wasn't in, however, so a cheery office assistant led me to a committee meeting that the Senator was attending. "It will be just a few minutes", she said, continuing to chat with me about the beauty and serenity of Montana. She had grown up in Great Falls or somewhere nearby, and missed the quiet open range and starry nights. I must have reminded her of what she was like before deciding to test the dirty waters of Washington politics. Looking back, I must have still embodied the innocence she wished she hadn't lost.

About five minutes later, Max scurried out and shook my hand as if I were the elected official he had traveled a thousand miles to meet. "So glad to finally meet you", he said. "How in the hell does he know who I am?" I thought. He didn't, of course. He was just politicking.

Max wasn't a good ole boy like Conrad Burns, his rival Republican from Montana, who said during his first campaign in 1988 that he would help single mothers by "[telling] them to find a husband". But Max was sleazy in his own right. His gaudy single-knot tie and wing-tip shoes caught my eye immediately. I remember wondering how long Mr. Baucus had been away from the Big Sky Country. I didn't really care. He was the Democrat I had come to see.

I asked him about Washington life, and we poked fun at Senator Conrad Burns, whom I had met earlier in the day. Whereas Max's busy over-packed office was full of citizens who seemed to care, Conrad's office was filled with wide leather couches and trophy animals that hung on his plush papered walls. We joked about Burns' assistants who were advising him on how he should vote on specific legislation even though they had never even seen Montana. I thought to myself, "Man, Democrats really are a lot cooler than Republicans". It didn't hurt that Max knew my uncle who ran a little grocery store in Lockwood, a small town outside of the city where I grew up. It made me think Max was one of us, a regular guy who represented regular folks. I let the used car salesman attire slide; the guy was all right.

My trip ended soon thereafter. I had met some interesting people, seen a lot of monuments and museums, and was enthralled with how the system actually worked. Or at least I thought I understood how it functioned. The runners, the lobbyists, the rookies, the senior congressional leaders, the reporters, and oh those interns. I thought I had it down. I couldn't wait to get home to tell my family what I'd learned, whom I'd met, and how Senator Baucus knew my dad's brother. I was even contemplating the best way for me to help his upcoming election campaign. As a Democrat enthusiast, I was much like Howard's Deaniacs, who canvassed my neighborhood daily with their cheeky grins and bouncy gaits. Yeah, I was annoying as hell.

It wasn't more than six months later that I was knocked to my senses by a sobering blow. I had read in the paper that Max Baucus had supported the North America Free Trade Agreement a few years back. By then, I was interested in environmental issues and came across the effects of NAFTA and the senators who supported it. Baucus was at the top of the hit list. I couldn't believe it.

Upon further exploration, I learned that Baucus sat on influential congressional committees, including Agriculture, Nutrition and Forestry, Environment and Public Works, and Finance and Joint Taxation. I learned how this man whom I had come to admire – for no real reason other than his bashing of a Republican – had succumbed to the interests of campaign contributors time and again. I found out how his seat on the Finance committee scored him bundles of cash from corporations I had never even heard of, including JP Morgan, Brown & Foreman, and Citigroup. I knew these guys weren't from Montana.

I also learned how my hero supported welfare reform, Fast Track, and President Clinton's Salvage Rider Act, all of which raped the Montana forests I loved so dearly. And a year later in college I read an article by Alexander Cockburn and Jeffrey St. Clair in the *Washington Post*, which disclosed how actor Robert Redford had campaigned for Baucus by dropping letters in the mailboxes of elite Hollywood liberals, hoping to entice them to donate money to the Montanan for his astute convictions for environmental justice. But as St. Clair and Cockburn put it so poignantly, "Across the length and breadth of Congress, it is impossible to uncover a more tenacious front-man for the mining, timber, and grazing industries ... it was Baucus who crushed the Clinton administration's timid effort to reform federal mining and grazing policies and terminate below-cost timber sales to big timber companies subsidized by the taxpayers". I was indignant. "How could he...?!" I pondered. "If the Democrats aren't saving our natural resources, who the hell is?"

That anger has festered in me to this day. Max Baucus may still be the most corporate-entrenched, conniving Democrat in Washington, and Montana has suffered tremendously as a result. Low employment. A broken public school system. A degraded natural environment. The exponential evaporation of the family farm. Montana's hurting, and the Democrats – most certainly Baucus – don't seem to give a damn.

The dangling tassels on Max's fancy wing-tip shoes will forever irk me. Those tassels and his decorative silk tie should have been the first sign that this politician didn't represent Montana. He was, after all, literally clad in the interests of the out-of-state corporations that lined his thick campaign coffers. I've hated the pretentious Wall Street pin stripes ever since Baucus' eye-opener.

I doubt that Max has ever hiked or driven through Montana's Yaak River basin, where a Forest Service timber sale has destroyed critical grizzly bear habitat. I'd bet he's never seen what the clear-cuts have done to the region's ecosystem, as tributaries have turned a pale yellow from mud and debris. And I can't imagine Baucus ever apologizing for the legislation he supported during the Clinton years that's to blame for it all. Many groups have challenged the illegalities of the outright pillage. But all of these suits have been defeated or dismissed because the salvage law gives the Forest Service "discretion to disregard entirely the effect on the grizzly bear". All this from the party I once belonged to.

I can't fathom that Baucus has sat down and spoken with the hundreds of poor single mothers in rural Montana who can't afford to put their kids in daycare because they are forced to work at places like Wal-Mart where they earn little more than minimum wage. I am sure they'd love to tell him how grateful they are for their newfound careers and Clinton's welfare reform that put them to work. Unlike many progressives who are preoccupied with the war in Iraq and U.S. foreign policy, these Montanans have more pressing concerns. They are turned off by politics because they have trouble keeping food in the fridge and buying holiday gifts for their kids. For most of us, it's a luxury to be politically active.

People continue to believe it's only the Republicans who have undermined everything progressives have fought for. I once believed this to be the case. I hated conservatives for their outright disregard for the little guy. But my short voyage out east as a teenager turned into a life lesson, teaching me that political affiliation means little when talking about real life consequences of compromising ideals. I think this is a lesson we must all keep in mind as many look to the Democrats, naively hoping that they will save us from the strangle of the neoconservatives' choke hold. Let's not allow fancy rhetoric or party loyalty to derail our need for real progressive change.

I wonder how my grandfather, who I'm told was a staunch Democrat, would feel about all this. He wasn't a flashy man but a hard-working North Dakotan farmer, who, as the story is told, even detested his neighbor for being what he called "one of those damned Republicans". Back then, although never progressive, Democrats stood for something, and were even elected to office because rural folk could discern the difference between a donkey and an elephant. I am convinced no such differences exist today, and I'm certain that my granddad would agree.

Senator Max Baucus will be in office until 2006, and he's not the only liberal impostor who will be. We are up against many. I guess I should give credit to Baucus for teaching me that Democrats aren't to be trusted anymore than Republicans. Thanks for the education, Max.

Chapter 10

"His many admirers in the press often call Senator John McCain, Republican from Arizona, seeker of his party's presidential nomination in 2000, a maverick. Since, in his substantive politics, he's impeccably orthodox, this shows how the term 'maverick' has gone down in the world."

Alexander Cockburn, Andrew Cockburn
and Jeffrey St. Clair
John McCain, Phony "Maverick"

Alexander Cockburn, Andrew Cockburn
and Jeffrey St. Clair

John McCain, Phony "Maverick"

S ENATOR JOHN McCAIN, REPUBLICAN FROM ARIZONA,
seeker of his party's presidential nomination in 2000, is
often called a maverick by his many admirers in the
press. Since, in his substantive politics, he's impeccably orthodox, this shows how the term "maverick" has gone down in the
world. These days, with the exception of Ron Paul, libertarian
Republican rep from Texas' 14th district, there simply aren't any
mavericks to be seen under the Capitol. So, "maverick", no.
Warmonger, yes. McCain, amid fierce competition, is the top
warmonger in Congress. In one rhetorical bombing run after
another, McCain has bellowed for "lights out in Belgrade" and
for NATO to "cream" the Serbs back at the close of the Nineties.
He was hot for war on Iraq.

McCain is often called a "war hero", a title adorning an
unlovely resume ranging from a father who was an admiral to the
son's graduation fifth from the bottom at the US Naval Academy,
where he earned the nickname "McNasty". McCain flew 23
bombing missions over North Vietnam, each averaging about
half an hour, total time ten hours and thirty minutes. For these
brief excursions the admiral's son was awarded two Silver Stars,
two Legions of Merit, two Distinguished Flying Crosses, three
Bronze Stars, the Vietnamese Legion of Honor and three Purple
Hearts. *US Veteran Dispatch* calculates our hero earned a medal an
hour, which is pretty good going. McCain was shot down over
Hanoi on October 26, 1967 and parachuted into Truc Boch Lake,
whence he was hauled by Vietnamese, and put in prison.

A couple of years later he was interviewed in prison camp by
Fernando Barral, a Spanish psychiatrist living in Cuba. The
interview appeared in *Granma* on January 24, 1970.

Barral's evaluation of McCain is quoted by Amy Silverman, author of many excellent pieces on McCain in the Phoenix-based *New Times* weekly. Here's how Barral described "the personality of the prisoner who is responsible for many criminal bombings of the people". Barral goes on, "He (McCain) showed himself to be intellectually alert during the interview. From a morale point of view he is not in traumatic shock. He was able to be sarcastic, and even humorous, indicative of psychic equilibrium. From the moral and ideological point of view he showed us he is an insensitive individual without human depth, who does not show the slightest concern, who does not appear to have thought about the criminal acts he committed against a population from the absolute impunity of his airplane, and that nevertheless those people saved his life, fed him, and looked after his health and he is now healthy and strong. I believe that he has bombed densely populated places for sport. I noted that he was hardened, that he spoke of banal things as if he were at a cocktail party."

McCain is deeply loved by the press. As Silverman puts it, "as long as he's the noble outsider, McCain can get away with anything it seems – the Keating Five, a drug-stealing wife, nasty jokes about Chelsea Clinton – and the pundits will gurgle and coo."

INDEED THEY WILL. WILLIAM SAFIRE, MAUREEN DOWD, RUSSELL Baker, the *New Yorker*, the *New York Times Magazine*, *Vanity Fair*, have all slobbered over McCain in empurpled prose. The culmination was a love poem from Mike Wallace on *60 Minutes*, who managed to avoid any inconvenient mention of McCain's close relationship with S & L fraudster Charles Keating, with whom the senator and his kids romped on Bahamian beaches. McCain was similarly spared scrutiny for his astonishing claim that he knew nothing of his wife's scandalous dealings. His vicious temper has also escaped rebuke.

McCain's escape from the Keating debacle was nothing short of miraculous, probably the activity for which he most deserves a medal. After all, he took more than $100,000 in campaign contributions from the swindler Keating between 1982 and 1988, while simultaneously log-rolling for Keating on Capitol Hill. In the same period McCain took nine trips to Keating's place in the Bahamas. When the muck began to rise, McCain threw Keating over the side, hastily reimbursed him for the trips and suddenly developed a profound interest in campaign finance reform.

The pundits love McCain because of his grandstanding on soft money's baneful role in politics, thus garnering for himself a reputation for willingness to court the enmity of his colleagues.

In fact colleagues in the Senate regard McCain as a mere grandstander. They know that he already has a big war chest left over from his last senatorial campaign, plus torrents of PAC money from the corporations that crave his indulgence, as chairman of the Senate Commerce Committee. Communications companies (US West, Bell South, ATT, Bell Atlantic) have been particularly effusive in McCain's treasury, as have banks, military contractors and UPS. They also know he has a rich wife.

McCain is the kind of Republican that liberals love: solid military credentials as a former POW, ever ready with acceptable sound-bites on campaign finance reform and other cherished issues. Thus it was that McCain drew enthusiastic plaudits some years ago when he rose in the Senate chamber to denounce the insertion of $200 million worth of pork in the military construction portion of the defense authorization bill. Eloquently, he spoke of the 11,200 service families on food stamps, the lack of modern weapons supplied to the military, the declining levels of readiness in the armed forces. Bravely, he laid the blame at the doors of his colleagues: "I could find only one commonality to these projects, and that is that 90 percent of them happened to be in the state or districts of members of the Appropriations

Committees." Sternly, in tones befitting a Cato or a Cicero, he urged his colleagues to ponder their sacred duty to uphold the defense of the Republic rather than frittering away the public purse on such frivolous expenditure: "We live in a very dangerous world. We will have some serious foreign policy crises. I am not sure we have the military that is capable of meeting some of these foreseeable threats, but I know that what we are doing with this $200 million will not do a single thing to improve our ability to meet that threat."

In the gallery, partisans of pork-free spending silently cheered while those who hoped to profit from portions of the $200 million gnashed their teeth in chagrin. Yet, such emotions were misplaced on either side. This was vintage McCain. Had he wished to follow words with deeds, he could have called for a roll call on the items he had just denounced so fervently. That way the looters and gougers would have had to place their infamy on the record. But no, McCain simply sat down and allowed the offending expenditure to be authorized in the anonymous babble of a voice vote ("All those in favor say Aye"). Had McCain really had the courage of his alleged convictions he could have filibustered the entire $250 billion authorization bill, but, inevitably, no such bravery was in evidence. Instead, when the $250 billion finally came to a vote, he voted for it.

This miserable display provides useful insights into the reason for McCain's ineffectiveness on issues such as campaign finance that have garnered him so much favorable publicity. A conservative senate staffer offers these observations on McCain's fundamental weakness of character: "the real question is why this senator did not use the strong leverage he has to insist that his 'ethical' position be incorporated into a major bill? After all, Senator McCain couched his concerns in issues of the highest national importance: readiness, modernization, and the military's ability to defeat the threats we face (whatever they are). 'Pragmatism' is the most commonly heard excuse. If McCain had made a pain out of himself in insisting on keeping the unneeded and wasteful pork out of the Pentagon authorization Bill, some people would argue he would have lost comity with his senate colleagues. They wouldn't respect him anymore; they would have been angry with him, because he kept them up late (it was about 10:30 pm), and they would have been embarrassed by his showing them up as pork-meisters. This would weaken his ability to get things done.

"This argument assumes politics in the US Senate is a popularity contest: if you want to get anything done around here, you have to go along and get along. Well, this place is a popularity contest, but it is supposed to be one with the voters, not one's colleagues. Besides, this place doesn't really operate that way. Here, they have contempt for fluffy show pieces. Show them you mean business, and you're someone who has to be dealt with (rather than a talk-only type), and you'll begin to get some results. Get ready for a fight, though, because there are some on the other side who are no pushovers. Obviously, Mr. McCain was not prepared to make that investment."

Chapter 11

"The big greens, all Democrats, get defeated on forests every time and every time it's by a wider margin. Is it mere ineptness? Or is something darker going on here? Is losing a reflex? Or are they throwing the game and blaming the loss on Bush and Republican ultras for their own political purposes?"

Michael Donnelly
One Wyden; Many Masters

Michael Donnelly
One Wyden; Many Masters

I N THESE DAYS OF BRAND POLITICS, ALL POLITICIANS MUST have a motto. For Ron Wyden, Oregon's senior US senator, it's the ecumenical slogan, "Standing up for ALL of Oregon". It's right there at the top of his recent press release proudly proclaiming his and Senator Dianne Feinstein's crucial role in persuading the US Senate to adopt their version of the deceptively titled Healthy Forests Initiative.

ALL Oregon? Hmmm? How does that rhetoric stack up to reality? Did ALL Oregon support this raid on our public lands? Hardly. Polls show that the majority of Oregonians opposed it. So, which Oregon does the senator represent? Maybe it's the Israeli lobby? Wyden's their number one senate PAC money recipient in a state that's two percent Jewish. Probably not.

Maybe it's the telecommunications industry? Again, Wyden's their number one PAC guy, as well. *The Oregon Business Journal* lists but one telecom with an Oregon headquarters.

So, again, probably not.

Could it be used car dealers? He's number three for them.

How about dentists? He's their number two man in the Senate.

Dietary supplements? Number three again. (No word on whether he's being called before the grand jury along with Barry Bonds.)

Perhaps the Sierra Club, which along with the League of Conservation Voters (LCV) has blindly endorsed the senator in every political race he's ever run.

Maybe the National Association of Police Organizations which made him their Senator of the Year?

Nope.

One has to go to Wyden's other number one senate PAC ranking – Big Timber! Yep. That's right. Ron Wyden hauled in more money from Timber PACs than any other senator the 2004 election season.

In fact, he hauled in more timber bucks than any other US politician, save one, George W. Bush. Now Bush will now sign into law what Wyden, himself, proudly calls the "Wyden/Feinstein Forest Compromise", although the environmental establishment, lapdogs of the Democratic Party, persists in calling it Bush's "Healthy Forests Initiative (HFI)." For Big Timber, Ron Wyden clearly has stood up. Perhaps Bush will hand him a souvenir pen after he signs the logging bill into law.

When one considers that in his long tenure as Big Timber's greatest friend, even former Republican Senator Mark O. Hatfield was never the industry's number one PAC recipient, the depth of the betrayal begins to register. At least with Hatfield, even though he is responsible for over 10 million acres of old growth stumps, he would always throw a morsel or two to conservationists. Big morsels. Wilderness Areas like Opal Creek, at that. Throughout his long career, Wyden has been responsible for precisely zero forest protection successes. Yet, he is portrayed as a champion of the green cause.

So how did this lifelong politician's vote come up for sale?

The story going round for decades in Oregon is that in 1974, as a young University of Oregon law grad, Wyden did a major venue shop of the entire West Coast looking for just the right congressional district to move to so as to fulfill his dad, writer Peter Wyden's, cradle-imprinted congressional hopes for him. Once the ambitious young Ron found the right district, Oregon's progressive Third, he quickly moved from Eugene to a Legal Aid position in Portland and the rest is history.

So how does Big Timber's number one guy get those LCV and Sierra Club endorsements?

Easy: the environmental movement has largely become a wholly owned subsidiary of the Democratic Party. Consider this: Wyden has an 80 percent positive rating from the League of Conservation Voters, which supposedly scores politicians on their environmental votes. But the ratings are rigged. Sure, Wyden casts the obligatory Nay on the annual shadow dance on oil drilling in the Arctic National Wildlife Refuge. He did support the great, under-appreciated (hey, he is *the* guy who brought an end to nuclear testing!), former Rep. Mike Kopetski's efforts to protect the magnificent Ancient Forests of Opal Creek. This action bought Wyden a lot of cover. Even when running against him in the primary fight for the disgraced Bob Packwood's senate seat, I couldn't bring myself to go after Wyden on the environment, simply because of Opal Creek. In retrospect, it was not such a bright move on my part.

But talking about not so bright moves, how is it that after a year of declaring "stopping Bush's HFI" to be their collective "Number One Priority" and raising some $5 million to fight it, the big greens were smoked in a lopsided 80-14 vote? Simple. They were backstabbed from within. Wyden and Feinstein (along with Montana's Max Baucus) did what Republican senators Trent Lott and Gordon Smith couldn't: they shepherded the logging bill past a potential senate filibuster. Bush unveiled it on August 22, 2002 and those darlings of the League of Conservation Voters, Wyden and Feinstein, sealed the deal and the fate of the forests a year later. This is what the combined forces of Big Green produced on their top priority.

How much did Wyden's vote cost? That number one ranking came cheap. He took in a mere $32,500 (Bush got $213,000). Methinks the Big Greens need some strategic rethinking. They could lay off but one of their incompetent staff and use the bloated salary to buy a few Wydens at that price.

The big greens get defeated on forests every time and every time it's by a wider margin. Is it mere ineptness? Or is something darker going on here? Is losing a reflex? Or are they throwing the game and blaming the loss on Bush and Republican ultras for their own political purposes? Those are the two choices: incompetence or collusion. When one follows Deep Throat's famous advice and looks at the money, here's what we find: not only is Wyden number one, other Democrats make up seven more of Big Timber's Sweet Sixteen, with Blanche Lincoln (LCV rating, 32 percent) at number four; Joe Lieberman (LCV, 88 percent) number six; Patty Murray (LCV, 76 percent) number ten; John Kerry (LCV, 92 percent) number eleven; Bob Graham (LCV, 64 percent) number twelve tied with Mary Landrieu (LCV, 20 percent) and John Edwards (LCV, 68 percent) at sixteen.

Lieberman, Kerry and Edwards failed to vote on the Wyden-Feinstein bill, just as they failed to vote on Bush's nomination of the slavishly pro-industry Mike Leavitt as head of the EPA, thus preserving their records of not recording any environmental votes in 2004! Sen. Hillary Clinton, who garnered lots of ink for her 9/11/03 "vow" to block Leavitt, sheepishly voted a month later to confirm him, as did most Democrats in an 88-8 vote. Rather sobering. And, yes, collusion is going on here. It's all about Big Greens covering for bad Democrats, pure and simple. When appalled activists met to discuss reprising the entertaining and extensively reported Weenie Roast they held outside Wyden's office after he went along with previous Big Timber "salvage" giveaways, the Sierra Club nixed the idea because "he's our friend". After the defeat on HFI, the Wilderness Society went public with their sentiment, telling the *Idaho Statesman* that the "bill offers workable solutions to forest problems, as long as the government follows through with its promises". In California, Wilderness Society staffer Jay Watson said it was a bill "we can work with". Talk about weenies!

Grassroots organizers, however, did show up at Wyden's office on Halloween, the day after the Senate bloodbath. They made their displeasure known and were able to get local media coverage of their outrage and the fact that big, old trees were still being cut a decade after the Big Greens declared it "our greatest victory" that Bill Clinton had "saved the Ancient Forest".

Ivan Maluski, dressed in a salmon outfit, said, "The bill that passed the Senate last night is a logging bill. It opens up 20 million acres and who knows how many of those are going to be in Oregon and a lot of that is going to be in the backcountry far away from homes and communities. The way we read some of the old growth provisions – it actually targets old growth forest for logging and that's really dangerous."

One thing one has to give the Big Greens credit for is that their original analysis of the provisions of the HFI was quite accurate. Instead of creating healthy forests, it's clearly a huge giveaway to Big Timber and Big Timber's more recent offshoot, privatized Big Fire prevention. Industry will be able to go after big green trees far from any human development. As Forest Service Chief Dale Bosworth has noted, it makes no economic sense otherwise. These folks have sold the notion that cutting the biggest, most fire-resistant trees will somehow make the forests less vulnerable to fire.

And Big Fire prevention, a highly unregulated industry that is totally dependent on there being fires and which often has seen its employees become the arsonists that start them, got an additional $760 million, pushing the total set aside for fire prevention to over $1.2 billion for the fiscal year. And, wait a minute. Yes, indeed, it becomes clearer. Over 80 percent of all the private companies in this industry are headquartered in Oregon. Under Wyden/Feinstein, these companies, many direct offshoots of timber firms, will become triple dippers: paid to "prevent" the fires with "fuel reduction projects", paid to fight the fires, and then paid for the "salvage and restoration logging" that inevitably follows. Big Fire benefits greatly from the senator-for-all-Oregon's compromise. But, just how effective is this industry? Who put out the California fires, anyway? Mother

Nature, as always – this time in the form of rain, mists and snow. Yet, Wyden still believes the best way to fight a fire is to smother it with federal dollar bills.

Even though Wyden has been named one of the dumbest members of Congress, he is something of an idiot savant when it comes to having his cake and eating it too. Wyden will go on to more timber PAC and other corporate money, yet he will continue to enjoy high LCV ratings and Sierra Club endorsements. Gordon Smith should cry foul. They have nearly identical records on National Forest policy (log more), yet Wyden pockets money from both Big Timber and Big Green.

Green Central will continue to blame their defeats on Bush and the Republicans. Gordon Smith will take on more principled stands than the craven Wyden. Senator-from-birth Ron Wyden will continue his "Standing up for ALL of Oregon's" ruling elites. One senator; many rich masters.

Chapter 12

"Santorum, the Mullah Omar of Pennsylvania, is a ridiculous spectacle but he can't be taken lightly. He is the slick-haired darling of the neo-cons, an obedient automaton that feverishly promotes their wildest fantasies without hesitation. When it comes to the Middle East, liberal Democrats race to co-sponsor legislation with him."

Jeffrey St. Clair
Santorum: That's Latin for Asshole

JEFFREY ST. CLAIR

Santorum: That's Latin for Asshole

RICK SANTORUM HAD ONLY BEEN IN THE SENATE FOR A few weeks when Bob Kerrey, then Senator from Nebraska, pegged him. "Santorum, isn't that Latin for asshole?" It was probably the funniest line the grim Kerrey ever uttered and it was on the mark, too. Such a stew of sleazy self-righteousness and audacious stupidity has not been seen in the senate since the days of Steve Symms, the celebrated moron from Idaho. In 1998, investigative reporter Ken Silverstein fingered Santorum as the dumbest member of congress in a story for *The Progressive*. Considering the competition of such titans as Inhofe of Oklahoma, that's an achievement of considerable magnitude.

Even Santorum's staff knows the senator is a vacuous boob prone to outrageous gaffes and outbursts of unvarnished bigotry. For years, they kept him firmly leashed, rarely permitting him to attend a press interview without a senior staffer by his side. They learned the hard way. While serving in the House, Santorum was asked by a reporter to explain why his record on environmental policy was so dreadful. Santorum replied by observing that the environment was of little consequence in God's grand plan. "Nowhere in the Bible does it say that America will be here 100 years from now". The reference was to the Rapture, which apparently is impending.

Santorum is the self-anointed prophet of family values on the Hill. He issues frequent jeremiads on the threats Hollywood poses to the "fabric of American culture". Such sermons are hard to swallow from a man with Santorum's resume. After all, before entering Congress Santorum worked as a lobbyist. His top client? The World Wrestling Federation.

But then the Republican leadership, apparently cruising along in self-destruct mode, elevated Santorum to the number three spot in the senate and his staff couldn't run interference for him anymore. The results were comically predictable. In the fall of 2003 Santorum wrote an op-ed for a Christian paper blaming the sexual molestation scandals in the Catholic Church on "the culture of liberalism". Surely, an omen that the senator from Pennsylvania wasn't quite ready for prime time.

So it came to pass that on April 7, Santorum sat down for an interview with AP reporter Lara Jordan. He should have been on his guard. After all, Jordan is married to Jim Jordan, who oversees John Kerry's presidential campaign. Kerry's wife, Teresa Heinz, despises Santorum. He inherited the senate seat left open when her previous husband, John Heinz, perished in a plane crash. "Santorum is critical of everything, indifferent to nuance, and incapable of compromise", Heinz said. This should have been a warning signal to Santorum that the interview with Jordan might be hostile terrain, but his intellectual radar remained inert.

After a brisk discussion of the degeneracy of American culture, the interview turned to the subject of the pending Supreme Court case on sodomy laws. Like many religious zealots, Santorum is obsessed not just with homosexuals but with visualizing the postures and physical mechanics of homosexual love. He seized on her question with an enthusiasm many Republicans reserve for discussions of the tax code.

"I have no problem with homosexuality", Santorum pronounced. "I have a problem with homosexual acts. As I would with acts of other, what I would consider to be, acts outside of traditional heterosexual relationships. And that includes a variety of different acts, not just homosexual. I have nothing, absolutely nothing against anyone who's homosexual. If that's their orientation, then I accept that. And I have no problem with someone who has other orientations. The question is, do you act upon those orientations? So it's not the person, it's the person's actions. And you have to separate the person from their actions". In the past, one of Santorum's staffers would have found some way to interrupt the interview and deftly muzzle the senator. But he was flying solo.

AP: "OK, without being too gory or graphic, so if somebody is homosexual, you would argue that they should not have sex?"

SANTORUM: "We have laws in states, like the one at the Supreme Court right now, that [have] sodomy laws and they were there for a purpose. Because, again, I would argue, they undermine the basic tenets of our society and the family. And if the Supreme Court says that you have the right to consensual sex within your home, then you have the right to bigamy, you have the right to polygamy, you have the right to incest, you have the right to adultery. You have the right to anything. Does that undermine the fabric of our society? I would argue yes, it does. It all comes from, I would argue, this right to privacy that doesn't exist in my opinion in the United States Constitution, this right that was created, it was created in *Griswold* – *Griswold* was the contraceptive case – and abortion. And now we're just extending it out. And the further you extend it out, the more you – this freedom actually intervenes and affects the family. You say, well, it's my individual freedom. Yes, but it destroys the basic unit of our society because it condones behavior that's antithetical to strong, healthy families. Whether it's polygamy, whether it's adultery, whether it's sodomy, all of those things, are antithetical to a healthy, stable, traditional family.

"Every society in the history of man has upheld the institution of marriage as a bond between a man and a woman. Why? Because society is based on one thing: that society is based on the future of the society. And that's what? Children. Monogamous relationships. In every society, the definition of marriage has not ever to my knowledge included homosexuality. That's not to pick on homosexuality. It's not, you know, man on child, man on dog, or whatever the case may be. It is one thing. And when you destroy that you have a dramatic impact on the quality."

At this point, even the unnerved reporter tried to rein in Santorum. "I'm sorry", Jordan interjected. "I didn't think I was going to talk about 'man on dog' with a United States senator, it's sort of freaking me out".

But Santorum was in full cry and there was no stopping him. "And that's sort of where we are in today's world, unfortunately", Santorum said. "The idea is that the state doesn't have rights to limit individuals' wants and passions. I disagree with that. I think we absolutely have rights because there are consequences to letting people live out whatever wants or passions they desire. And we're seeing it in our society".

There you have it. A case study in the politics of pathological homophobia. Despite outcries from gay Republicans, Bush stood by Santorum in his hour of media martyrdom: "The president believes the senator is an inclusive man", Ari Fleischer informed the press. "And that's what he believes". Santorum's pal Tom DeLay, the pest exterminator-turned-Republican House Majority Leader, was ebullient. He called Santorum's remarks "courageous".

Trent Lott must have been snickering in the senate cloakroom.

Santorum, the Mullah Omar of Pennsylvania, is a ridiculous spectacle but he can't be taken lightly. He is the slick-haired darling of the neo-cons, an obedient automaton that feverishly promotes their wildest fantasies without hesitation.

Undeterred by the First Amendment, Santorum introduced legislation that aims to limit criticism of Israel in colleges and universities that receive federal money. And his passion for Israel is so profound that it obviates even his rancid homophobia. When it comes to the Middle East, liberal Democrats race to co-sponsor legislation with him. In 2003, Santorum and Barbara

Boxer teamed up to introduce the Syria Accountability Act, which would inflict trade sanctions on Syria like those which gripped Iraq for 12 years, killing nearly one million children. Talk about family values.

Sure, Santorum is an asshole. But he's not one of a kind.

Chapter 13

"Racicot, whose hair is as delicately managed as John Kerry's, may look benign next to the frightful visages of Rove and Rumsfeld, but he's a ruthless politician who is as far to the right as anyone in the Bush inner circle. Just ask those who know him best: the people of Montana."

Jeffrey St. Clair
Marc Racicot: Bush's Main Man

JEFFREY ST. CLAIR
Marc Racicot: Bush's Main Man

WHEN THE FLORIDA RECOUNT FIASCO WAS IN FULL-throttle, the Bush team called in one of its top fixers to deal with the media and help put the finishing touches on the brusque strategy that helped seal the election. That man was Marc Racicot, the former governor of Montana. Many thought he would be rewarded for his efforts with a top post in the Bush White House. Although he was on the short list for both Secretary of the Interior and Attorney General, Racicot ended up in the cushy post as head of the Republican National Committee, where his deft fundraising abilities fattened the RNC vaults with a record $250 million in soft money contributions for the 2002 election cycle.

Racicot didn't just sit on that mountain of cash; he used it like a MOAB bomb on Democrats. He is credited along with Karl Rove with devising the media strategy that yielded such great triumphs for the Republicans in the 2002 elections.

In early June, 2003, Bush tapped Racicot as the chairman of his reelection campaign and soon the corporate loot was pouring into the Bush campaign coffers. It was an astute choice. Although his name is hard to pronounce (Ross-Co), Racicot presents a kinder media presence than the other visigoths in the Bush camp. One Republican staffer called him "the white Colin Powell, the only two Bush advisers with any kind of sex appeal."

Racicot, whose hair is as delicately managed as John Kerry's, may look benign next to the frightful visages of Rove and Rumsfeld, but he's a ruthless politician who is as far to the right as anyone in the Bush inner circle. Just ask those who know him best: the people of Montana.

Racicot served as governor of Montana from 1994 through 2000, where he slashed taxes, carried water for big timber, deregulated the state's electric utilities and moaned ceaselessly about the oppressive hand of the federal government. Prior to that Racicot served two terms as attorney general for the Big Sky state.

These days Montana's once robust economy is in ruins. The current governor, Racicot's bumbling protégé Judy Martz, gets most the blame for the crisis and lumbers along with an approval rating of 23 percent. But Racicot's savage economic policies laid the foundations for the wreck that now plagues the state: record deficits, bankrupt schools and a senescent economy.

While Racicot slashed services and taxes, he also funneled what little money remained in the Montana treasury into costly projects that benefited political donors. For example, Racicot spent tens of millions of dollars on a new software system for the state government that was supposed to minutely track agency budgets and expenditures. Nearly a decade and $50 million later, the system still doesn't function and the workings of state's budget (now deep in the red) remains as opaque as the rituals of Eleusis.

Although the state of Montana was veering toward bankruptcy, Racicot sank $100 million into the construction of new prisons, which were built by political donors. The problem was that Montana was one of the few states with an overcapacity of prison beds. The prisons went up anyway and despite a slate of harsh new laws passed under Racicot and Martz to lock up more Montanans the new prisons remain underbooked. Now, Montana is desperately looking to rent out its empty cells to other states.

His cavalier approach to the state's health care services was even more disastrous. Racicot pushed through a $400 million scheme to privatize Montana's mental health care system. But less than two years after it was put into place, the new program collapsed, pushing schizophrenics and other patients out onto the streets and off needed medications. The state is now faced with recreating a system that Racicot destroyed.

When Montana's schools began to falter from the budget squeeze, Racicot offered a quick fix: log off the remaining old growth on state lands and cycle the receipts to the schools. This scheme, dubbed clearcuts for classrooms by local environmentalists, ravaged Montana's forests, but did almost nothing to help the state's beleaguered school system. Using the same rationale, Racicot also began selling off state park and forestlands near urban areas to his corporate cronies for shopping centers, office buildings and subdivisions.

Montana once enjoyed the toughest clean water laws in the country. Racicot dismantled them in 1995 when he signed a bill backed by mining and oil companies which raised limits on the discharge of toxins and carcinogens into Montana's streams, allowed corporations the right to police their own conduct and at the behest of the coal methane producers expanded the luxury to foul groundwater to the very boundaries of polluter's property.

This was followed by Racicot's big gift to the strip-mining lobby. Despite the fact that Montana, which bears the historical scars of the strip-and-run coal companies, is the only state in the nation whose constitution requires the reclamation of all lands disturbed by mining, Racicot signed into a law a measure that exempts open pit mines from any responsibility to restore the mess they make, often contaminated with cyanide and other toxic debris.

But perhaps the biggest fiasco of Racicot's tenure as governor was his role in deregulating Montana's electric utilities, which allowed Montana Power Company to sell off its generating stations, dams, powerlines and water rights to PPL (Pennsylvania Power and Light). In exchange, Montana ratepayers saw their utility bills soar by more than 50 percent, from one of the lowest in the nation to the highest.

Racicot forged a close friendship with Bush in 1995, when the two men began working together on anti-regulatory initiatives for the Western Governors' Association and the National Governors' Association. The relationship between the two governors proved so cozy that there was speculation in Montana that Bush might pick Racicot as his running mate in the 2000. Ultimately, Dick Cheney picked himself for that position and the golden boy from Montana went to work in the DC office of Bracewell & Patterson, a Houston law firm with close ties to Bush specializing in advancing the agendas of oil and gas companies.

One of Racicot's chief clients during those tumultuous early days of the Bush administration was in dire need of a well-placed hand: Enron. Even after Racicot was selected to head the RNC, he refused to drop Enron as a client. His efforts to protect Enron during its time of tribulation certainly paid off for the company's executives. While Martha Stewart was facing federal charges over a $200,000 stock deal, Enron executives Ken Lay and Jeffrey Skilling, who bilked investors out of billions, enjoyed afternoons on the most exclusive golf courses in Houston.

After Racicot became chairman of the RNC he moved his office to the party's headquarters a couple of blocks from the White House. Even though he rarely went into the law office and had no official roster of clients, Racicot continued to pull down a six-figure paycheck from Bracewell & Paterson.

"I have certainly provided advice and counsel to some private people with private business activities that have not been governmentally related", Racicot said. "So I have done some things, but it has been very limited. So as a result of that I have honored the terms of the employment agreement and they were in such a frame of mind that they thought (leading the Republican Party) was something constructive for me to be engaged in and they acquiesced to my involvement."

The head of the Bush campaign sees no reason to recuse himself from such easy money now.

Chapter 14

The late Senator Paul Wellstone remains a liberal icon. Everything a Democrat should be. Shortly before his campaign plane nosedived into the north Minnesota woods in 2002, *CounterPunch* ran this still useful bout of icon-bashing by a Minnesotan Green.

Jeff Taylor
Paul Wellstone: a Liberal Icon?

Paul Wellstone: a Liberal Icon?

WHEN GREENS TALK TO EACH OTHER ABOUT HOW they're disappointed with Senator Paul Wellstone, you rarely hear criticism of his decision to break the term limits pledge he made in 1990 and reiterated in 1996. You're much more likely to hear references to Wellstone's support for the "Defense of Marriage Act" (1996) or his support for various military actions unrelated to the defense of our country (1992-2002). Some Greens see the breaking of Wellstone's promise as a minor thing, as something which should not be highlighted during the 2002 campaign because Wellstone simply changed his mind based on changed circumstances.

I don't see it that way. I think it's closely related to one of the most important values of the Green Party: grassroots democracy. Term limits is not a new concept. In ancient Athens, citizens made the laws themselves and every year they chose new administrators among themselves by using a lottery system. Admittedly, this system was flawed women and slaves were not citizens but it was an early attempt at democracy ("rule by the common people").

In the 1790s, Thomas Jefferson lamented that the new U.S. Constitution did not include mandatory "rotation in office". Populists throughout the past 200 years have held to the ideal of our representatives being citizen legislators, rather than a permanent class of professional politicians. In the early 1990s, Ralph Nader advocated term limits for politicians as part of his "toolbox of democracy" (Concord Principles).

There's an interesting book about the 1990 Minnesota senate race called *Professor Wellstone Goes to Washington*. Today, Senator Wellstone doesn't want to leave. Who can blame him? He makes

$150,000 a year (plus perks) and he's a member of one of the most prestigious and powerful groups in the world. That's not the whole story, of course. It's too cynical. I think Wellstone also wants to make the world a better place (in a bleeding-heart, mushy-headed, big-government, Hubert-Humphrey sort of way).

Even if we disagree with Wellstone's perspective or methods, he still deserves some credit for having aims more noble than accumulating personal power or doing favors for rich campaign contributors. That's commendable and it sets him apart from most officeholders in Washington. But there's one problem with extending this scenario year after year: Wellstone has become a professional politician. How long does he need to carry out his political goals? When he entered the Senate, he promised to use his position as a rallying spot for progressive, grassroots activists across the nation. That hasn't happened. The true story is less romantic.

Here's a case study to use when looking at the corrupting effects of hanging onto power for too long: Senator Wellstone and the use of the U.S. military in pursuit of the American Empire ("Policeman of the World", "New World Order", or whatever euphemism you prefer). Wellstone showed early promise as a vocal critic of George I's war for oil (and missile corporations and Saudi bases). Six years later, amid a reelection struggle, Wellstone minimized his peace-making efforts. *The Minneapolis Star Tribune* reported, "He notes that he was in favor of sending the troops [to Saudi Arabia] but objected to sending them into war before all alternatives had been pursued". (ST, 10-21-96) In other words, if sanctions had been tried for a while and Iraqi troops remained in Kuwait, then he would have supported the war for oil and other Bush objectives (democracy was obviously not one of them, since Kuwait and Saudi Arabia were both ruled by dictators).

Wellstone showed limited opposition to the military action of a Republican president, but when it came to Bush's Democratic successor, Wellstone was a virtual cheerleader. He supported every single Clinton troop deployment, missile launch, and bomb drop: Somalia (1992), Haiti (1994), Bosnia (1995), Iraq (1998), and Kosovo (1999).

Paul Wellstone's admiration for Hubert Humphrey is another possible explanation for his evolution into a supporter of continual U.S. military intervention in other countries (always in a context of little or no threat to U.S. citizens). Humphrey had his good points, but his brand of liberalism was pragmatic and largely based on his own emotional personality, not on constitutional principles or spiritual values. This being the case, whenever a president couched some imperialistic endeavor in nice-sounding, humanitarian language, Humphrey was pleased as punch to give his enthusiastic support to the mission. So, you had him endorsing interventions in Guatemala and the Dominican Republic and the war in Vietnam.

Like Humphrey, Wellstone tends to support a foreign policy pursued mostly for the benefit of transnational corporations and wealthy Americans whenever it's cloaked in idealistic rhetoric. That's a really unfortunate tendency. It's unfortunate for middle class Americans who pay burdensome taxes for these military "chess games"; it's unfortunate for the men and women in uniform who put their lives on the line for veiled, less-than-noble policies; and it's unfortunate for the many innocent people in other countries who are maimed and killed during these endeavors. Playing the long-established game of throwing some verbal crumbs to the voting base of their party, Democratic presidents are especially adept at using warm-and-fuzzy words – "I feel your pain" on a global scale – to justify power-and-profit policies. Ever hopeful of the good intentions of party colleagues, Wellstone signs off on all of these misuses of the military. For example, it apparently never occurred to him that our government's "feed the hungry" military mission in Somalia might have had something to do with oil exploration and exploitation rights granted to Conoco, Amoco, and Chevron before civil war rendered those rights unusable.

Turning to domestic policy, another case study comes to mind. Many liberals were disappointed when Wellstone voted for the "Defense of Marriage Act" passed by a Republican-controlled Congress and signed by President Clinton in 1996. Regardless of the merits of the bill, it has to be conceded that the idea of Clinton acting as the nation's "defender of marriage" is laughable! The same could probably be said for many of the sanctimonious members of Congress, including House Speaker Newt Gingrich. Gay and lesbian activists were stunned in June 1996 when Wellstone announced at a gay-sponsored fundraiser he "personally opposes same sex marriages" and was considering voting for the "Defense of Marriage" bill which would deny federal recognition of them. It seemed completely out of character for the "enlightened, progressive politician.

We might be able to piece together an explanation from the news story. *The Star Tribune* noted, "He faces reelection this fall in a race that is a top target nationally for Republicans". Two sentences later, the reporter says, "Wellstone shocked the crowd when he said he was raised to believe that marriage was reserved for the union of one man and one woman". This was the first his gay supporters had heard of this basic belief. Presumably, Wellstone was also raised to believe that romance and sex should be between one man and one woman, but that hadn't stopped him from unreservedly supporting gay rights throughout his years as a college teacher, political activist, and office holder.

If there was some political calculation in the Wellstone move – and it's hard to believe there wasn't some – it paid off, as you can see from this *Star-Tribune* headline three days later: "Gay Leaders Say They Still Back Wellstone" (ST, 6-8-96). Partly out of

over-privileged self-interest and partly out of the political equiv-
alent of battered-spouse syndrome, leaders of the Democratic
Party's core constituencies almost always stick with the
Democrat in an election, regardless of how much neglect,
humiliation, and mistreatment they've suffered at the hands of
that politician. It's one reason the Democratic Party will never
change. The only people in a position to force that change are
either too sold-out or too scared to take real action. The
Wellstone campaign knew that in 1996.

Some party activists and gay leaders openly acknowledged
Wellstone's cynicism, as they rushed to his side and made the
requisite excuses for his disappointing behavior. A Democratic-
Farmer-Labor (DFL) activist at Wellstone's gay-sponsored
fundraiser told a reporter, "This was a sophisticated crowd. He
could have told them that he was considering signing [sic] the
bill because he couldn't afford to have the religious right attack
him on that issue, that he needed those suburban middle class
voters. I think they would have accepted that".

Taking agility to new levels of mastery, a leader of the
Human Rights Campaign made the assertion that the whole
purpose of the "Defense of Marriage" bill was to "divide Senator
Wellstone from an important part of his constituent base" and
that gays and lesbians "should not be tricked". It's not that the
legislation was introduced by those genuinely fearful that the
"sacred institution" of marriage was under attack by a growing
movement at the state level. It's not that Wellstone betrayed his
principles for political gain (figuring he was in a win-win situation since he wouldn't alienate the majority of culturally conservative voters and would retain the support of most gay and
lesbian voters). No, the bill was "designed precisely to drive
people like Senator Wellstone out of Congress" and he was
smart enough to not fall into the trap. He avoided the trap by
moving toward an anti-gay rights position. That was a good
move, according to this gay rights leader. Even in 1996 the whole

world revolved around Wellstone and access to politicians like him by quasi-liberal interest group leaders.

When he announced his final decision to vote for the "Defense of Marriage" bill, Wellstone referred to gays who disagreed with his position, saying, "I've said to them, I don't think we should change the definition of marriage. It is the central institution of American life. You reach a certain consensus in society, and no court decision is going to change that". (ST, 9-10-96) When it comes to social consensus and court decision, you could say the exact same thing about *Brown v. Board of Education* (1954) which outlawed public school segregation or *Roe v. Wade* (1973) which legalized abortion in all 50 states. It's seemingly glib comments like this – from a man with a PhD in political science! – which make me question either Wellstone's knowledge or integrity. You can debate the merits (separately) of the nationwide social consensus for segregation in the 1940s, or against abortion in the 1960s, but the fact is judges stepped in and overruled popular opinion – and Wellstone approves of that judicial rejection of majority rule. Why is he inconsistent when it comes to same sex marriage? Since when did he become a champion of biblically-based popular sovereignty over politically-correct judicial tyranny? That's out of character for a darling of the limousine-liberal set. It's another indication that he was at least partly playing politics with the issue.

In 1996, Wellstone did not just have Minnesota voters in mind. If he was able to win reelection, he had thoughts of running for President. Six months after voting for the "Defense of Marriage Act", word was being spread that Wellstone might run for the 2000 Democratic presidential nomination. That may have been an additional factor in his support for the federal ban on same sex marriage. He would have seriously hurt his chances of attracting support in the primaries in culturally conservative areas of the country if he'd taken an unpopular, controversial position on a wedge issue like gay marriage. In the end,

Wellstone decided to opt out of the presidential race, but his national ambitions were probably another factor in his surprising 1996 position.

Let's compare Wellstone's privately-held beliefs about the sanctity of heterosexual marriage with a couple other progressive politicians who believed in the sanctity of human life. In the 1960s and 1970s, Senator Mark Hatfield (R-OR) and Senator Harold Hughes (D-IA) were prominent liberals in Washington. Both men were pro-life. I say "pro-life" instead of "anti-abortion" or "anti-choice" because they were consistently supportive of human life almost to the point of pacifism. They were Christians, but they were not Catholics and their opposition to legalized abortion did not come from a seemingly arbitrary edict of a patriarchal religious hierarchy.

In addition to being founded on a belief in nonviolence, their opposition to abortion was tied to a belief that it was being promoted as a classist and racist tool by wealthy population controllers uninterested in supplying deeper, juster solutions to the problems of poverty and inequality. You may disagree with their position, but it was publicly discussed, thoroughly explained, and consistently held (regardless of election dates and opinion polls). By 1973, Hatfield and Hughes had developed well-earned reputations as statesmen in progressive circles. They had been early opponents of the Vietnam War and outspoken critics of capital punishment. Although it was unusual for evangelical Christians to attempt a literal application of the Sermon on the Mount to public policy, by so doing, Hatfield and Hughes had drawn national attention to a nonviolent ethic reminiscent of the Quakers and Mennonites. So no one was surprised when they criticized *Roe v. Wade*. They had existing reputations as advocates for human life – and they hadn't been taking contributions from the Population Council, Planned Parenthood, and NARAL.

In complete contrast, Paul Wellstone's opposition to same sex marriage seemed to come out of nowhere and then disappeared just as quickly. There were no prior allusions to social norms coming out of his family or personal morality coming out of his religion relating to the limits of homosexual legitimation. There were no subsequent attempts to change the minds of gay activists or write the principle into the party platform.

Now, in 2002, we're told by Wellstone apologists that he had to vote for Bush's war in Afghanistan (which took the lives of thousands of civilians without bringing the 9-11 criminals to justice) and the misnamed "Patriot Act" (which should have been called the Big Brother is Watching You Act). If Wellstone had voted against these things, it would have been political suicide in an election year, we're told. Is there anything Wellstone believes in deeply enough that he's willing to risk losing his Senate seat? I guess it can't be said that he would rather be right than be senator. The irony is, as his integrity erodes, he'll lose more and more votes from those who care about integrity – and eventually he'll be neither right nor senator. Then what will he have to show for his opportunism?

Breaking a term limits promise is not just an abstract thing. It has practical consequences. When a politician chooses to dishonor that pledge, it's indicative of a deeper problem. That's why he's more and more apt to do other surprising and upsetting things – like endorsing every overseas military attack pushed by a Democratic president, turning his back on the gay rights agenda when it becomes a liability on the eve of an election, and supporting a Republican president's war policies and civil liberties infringements. If Wellstone's lease on power is renewed, you can expect more of the same.

Shortly after Wellstone announced that he was breaking his term limits promise, the University of Minnesota's Hubert H. Humphrey Institute senior fellow Joe Nathan wrote a newspaper column entitled "A Time for Breaking Promises" (*Rochester Post-*

Bulletin, 2-14-01). Nathan says, "I agree that Wellstone changed his mind and broke a promise. But I think breaking a commitment to the people who elected you sometimes is not only acceptable, but brave". Spoken like a true political scientist! Sad to say, most of my colleagues in the field of American government have a decidedly elitist slant. Lacking political power and popular influence themselves, they fawn over those who have these qualities. Thus, when politicians break promises by raising taxes on the common people and giving themselves pay raises, they're almost always hailed by political scholars for their "courage".

It really doesn't take much courage to be cynical, untrustworthy, and dishonorable. Experienced politicians know they can act like that and usually get away with it because the attention span of the average American voter is very short. By the time election day rolls around, if the betrayal hasn't already been forgotten, it can be neutralized by emphasizing some secondary wedge issue or raising the spectre of the bogeyman ("If you don't vote for X, you'll get Y – then you'll really be sorry!"). Plus, you have the "experts" on the editorial page and NPR telling the "educated" voter that the betrayal was really a brave act of statesmanship. Given these conditions, it's very difficult to hold a politician to his or her word.

Nathan continues: "In general we should keep promises. But sometimes circumstances change. If you can be more helpful by breaking a promise, you should do it". More helpful to whom? To one's self? No, Nathan says he supports Wellstone because "he can help more Minnesotans by staying in Congress – at least for another six years". Why only six years? If he stays for another thirty-six years, think of the seniority he'll build up and the pork he'll be able to deliver for the state! Using Nathan's logic that longevity in office is desirable for a constituency, then why not have members of the U.S. Senate chosen for life (à la the U.S. Supreme Court)? That would give everyone plenty of time to develop the experience needed to grapple with the difficult issues of our nation, the freedom to rise above partisan pressures, and the invulnerability to bravely break lots of promises. Of course, Nathan's logic of longer-is-better applies only to those select politicians who happen to agree with his beliefs. In other words, Strom Thurmond and Jesse Helms don't qualify.

Nathan concludes that it will be helpful for Wellstone to continue in office for at least six more years. But what about the substantial portion of the state which did not vote for Wellstone in 1996? Will they be helped by Wellstone's continuation in Washington? What about the malcontents who are so gauche that they expect politicians to live up to their promises – regardless of changing circumstances? Will they be helped by Wellstone's reelection and the accompanying reinforcement of his cynical behavior? In defending promise-breaking, Nathan points out that "sometimes circumstances change". No duh! Circumstances always change. That's a given. The question is, How will a politician choose to respond to the changing circumstances? With integrity or opportunism? With public service or self service? With commitment or betrayal?

The changing circumstances rationale first used by Wellstone and echoed by apologists like Nathan is probably specious anyway. Wellstone didn't groom anyone within the DFL to succeed him after making and remaking his no-third-term pledge. That strongly suggests that he had no intention of keeping his promise. Wellstone continued to raise campaign money and passed up the opportunity to publicly promote a successor in 1997, 1998, 1999, and 2000. Four years passed between his second election and the supposedly crucial changing of circumstances (Bush elected and the Senate evenly divided). This would lead an objective observer to suspect, if not conclude, that Wellstone never had any intention of retiring upon the conclusion of his second term.

Paul Wellstone became a professional politician. There are certain groups which had a vested interest in keeping Wellstone in power, namely (A) the quasi-liberal interest group leaders who make a good living off talking about the problems of others and exploiting their fears and (B) the corporate-funded Democratic Party which finds it useful to have a tame "liberal" on board to point to whenever Ralph Nader begins his siren song. The sad truth for progressives and populists is that Wellstone as a presence in Washington just isn't that important. He hasn't lived up to his promise. He hasn't had much impact. He's shifted his goal from universal, single-payer health insurance (a concrete, measurable goal) to helping people (an abstract goal which requires endless terms in office). His new, fuzzier goal gets corrupted not only by partisanship and gullibility but by one of the time-tested truisms of political science: power corrupts. He's no longer the new person in Washington, bringing fresh ideas and real-life experiences to the cynical and surreal atmosphere of Capitol Hill and K Street. Now he's part of that culture. Maybe not as debased as most, but still immersed.

Breaking his promise to serve only two terms isn't the real problem. It's a symptom. Wellstone the populist fighter lives on only in memory, stump speeches, and slick TV ads (many paid for by DFL soft money). Wellstone can't claim to be a man of great integrity. He's not that different from all the other politicians who call themselves "public servants" while they mostly serve themselves, their friends, and their pet causes. Wellstone may still be a cut above most national politicians, but he's squandered the promise with which he began. His loss of integrity will cost him votes – and perhaps his office. That's not the Green Party's fault. It's partly because Wellstone has chosen to tie his destiny to a corrupt and arrogant Democratic Party.

The Senator can't hardly run on the slogan "Paul Wellstone: Just Another Politician Trying to Hang Onto His Job", so the race is cast in portentous, almost apocalyptic terms. "Wellstone has to win to keep a Democratic majority in the Senate". "Wellstone is Bush's #1 target". "If Wellstone loses, it's the end of liberal civilization as we know it". Yeah, right. How is Wellstone's reliably Democratic vote any different from those of Tim Johnson or Bob Torricelli? When he does swim against the Democratic current, he's casting a symbolic vote which doesn't accomplish anything beyond bolstering his threadbare maverick image. If his one vote would make a real difference – against the interests of the Democratic establishment – he'd probably knuckle under with a self-deluded explanation.

That's what it's come to. Wellstone is pliant in relation to party leaders and he himself is not a leader of any organized movement. That makes him ineffective. When's the last time he stopped a Democratic president from doing something bad? Or tried to change his party's national platform in a major way? Or led a filibuster which stopped a big piece of bad legislation? Or affected the outcome of a presidential election? Or endorsed a progressive Republican? Or tried to start a third party? Or tried to stop a war?

Let's face it: Paul Wellstone is no Robert La Follette or Burton Wheeler or Jeannette Rankin or Wayne Morse or Fannie Lou Hamer. They were men and women who didn't bluster with populist rhetoric on the campaign trail but privately schmooze with the Manhattan/Beverly Hills elite and go along with the Washington power brokers when push comes to shove. They owed their jobs to the local voters, were pariahs within their own national parties, and repeatedly risked their careers for progressive principles. In contrast, Wellstone has left himself wide open to the charge that his 12 years in the Senate have been "full of sound and fury, signifying nothing". That's not much of a legacy.

The national Democratic Party had no agenda. It meekly followed President Bush's agenda. Bombing of Afghanis – partly to install a friendly and stable government to foster an oil consortium's plans to build a Central Asian pipeline through the country? Sure! Legislation which gives the President and national security apparatus unprecedented power to spy on U.S. citizens and violate constitutional guarantees during times of (undeclared) war? Sure! Alternative visions for America, other than quibbling about budget numbers on domestic programs and tinkering with foreign policy strategies? Nope! Genuine debate over public policy ends, not just means? Nope!

Let's say that deep down Wellstone really is the same friend-of-the-people he was in 1990. If he had chosen to honor his pledge, think of the freedom he would have had during his entire second term to vote his conscience and serve his constituents. He could have groomed a successor for 2002 more electable than himself – one without so much baggage and polarization. He might have run for governor of Minnesota and actually had a chance to implement all of his idealistic notions. For example, real campaign finance and health care reforms are more possible at the state level. And he would have given Minnesotans a much better DFL choice than Roger Moe, who exemplifies the discredited system of entrenched power. But, no, placing his own ambition and comfort above the well-being of the people, Wellstone pushed honor and all other considerations aside in pursuit of continued power at the federal level.

Taking a larger view of the world, and of history, we can see that it makes little difference whether Paul Wellstone remains in the Senate or not. His record is just not that distinguished. Despite his grassroots background and exciting campaign in 1990, he became a practitioner of the same old crap. Instead of recognizing value in life beyond the Beltway, he's launched a gratuitous, unprincipled, and selfish third campaign. I'm guessing that Senator Wellstone is surrounded by yes-men and yes-women who enjoy the high life in D.C. and want to retain a foothold in their fiefdom of power. They're not going to tell him it's time to go home. The union bosses, self-anointed demographic leaders, and direct-mail fearmongers who enjoy rubbing elbows with the famous and powerful aren't going to tell him he should keep a promise made in the heat of a campaign. Barbra Streisand isn't going to tell him he needs to play by the rules of average Minnesotans.

Term limits can be discussed in fancy historical and theoretical ways. The ill effects of entrenched power can be noted, ranging from negative personality traits to increased policy deficiencies. But regular rotation in office – whether self-imposed or voter-imposed – isn't hard to understand. It's really quite simple. Most of us learned it as kids, when our parents told us, "You've had your turn. Now you have to let someone else have a turn". Or, in the more blunt phrasing of one kid to another: "Quit hogging it!"

Chapter 15

"'You are the greatest fundraiser in the history of the universe.'"

Jeffrey St. Clair
The Political Business of Terry McAuliffe

Jeffrey St. Clair

The Political Business
of Terry McAuliffe

I N MAY 1999, THE LABOR DEPARTMENT BROUGHT SUIT
against Jack Moore and John Grau, charging the two men
with mismanaging the pension fund for the International
Brotherhood of Electrical Workers. Moore was the longtime secretary of the union, while Grau was the vice-president of the
National Electrical Contractor's Association, which was partner
in the fund. At issue was a series of sweetheart real estate deals
in central Florida, which regulators labeled "imprudent", and
cost the fund money. Moore and Grau eventually settled the case
for more than six figures. The union was forced to kick in
another $5 million to cover the losses to the pension fund. The
person at the center of the scandal, however, made out in the
deal very well, indeed. His name: Terry McAuliffe, now head of
the DNC.

McAuliffe met Moore in 1988, when both were raising
money for the doomed presidential bid of Dick Gephardt. They
became close friends, allies in a campaign to redesign the
Democratic Party into a more moderate political vessel, along
the lines of the pre-Reagan Republicans. Moore controlled the
$6 billion IBEW pension fund and had a reputation for investing
money in businesses run by friends and political cronies.

So it was that in November 1990, McAuliffe approached
Moore and his friend Grau with a proposal for a real estate part-
nership in central Florida with an investment company called
American Capital Management, which McAuliffe owned with
his wife Dorothy. The deal involved the purchase of the
Woodland Square Shopping Center and five apartment com-
plexes outside Orlando, Florida. It was a lopsided partnership.
The pension fund put up $39 million to purchase the property.

McAuliffe shelled out $100, yet he and his wife enjoyed 50 percent ownership in the project. He eventually parlayed his $100 investment into a $2.45 million profit.

Fresh from this triumph, McAuliffe approached Moore with a new proposal. He asked Moore to dip into the pension fund one more time for $6 million so that he could purchase a parcel of land south of Orlando called Country Run, which McAuliffe planned to subdivide into 500 single-family homes. Moore obliged and loaned McAuliffe the money. The development soon proved to be a bust. Only half the homes were built and many of them didn't sell. Years passed, but McAuliffe never bothered to make a single payment to the pension fund on the loan. According to Labor Department records, McAuliffe was in default from December 1992 through October 1997. The managers of the pension fund never demanded payment or called in the loan. The only collateral they had required was the nearly worthless Country Run property itself.

Eventually, McAuliffe found a buyer for the property and repaid the loan. But the aroma of the deals attracted the attention of the Labor Department, which had been looking into the looting of worker pension funds. In May of 1999, the agency brought a suit against Moore and Grau for mismanagement of the fund. Both eventually settled, agreeing to six figure fines, and resigned their positions. The IBEW was compelled to reimburse the pension fund to the tune of five million dollars. The Labor Department didn't have any authority to go after McAuliffe. That was up to the Clinton Justice Department and they took a pass. He wasn't sued or otherwise inconvenienced. So a labor fund got looted and Terry McAuliffe got very rich.

This wasn't the only time McAuliffe steered a labor union toward dangerous legal and financial shoals. In 1996, McAuliffe helped devise a political money-cycling scheme that led to the downfall of several leaders of the Teamster's Union, including the union's reform-minded president Ron Carey and his political director William Hamilton. At Hamilton's trial on corruption charges, Richard Sullivan, the former director of finance for the Democratic National Committee, testified that McAuliffe asked Sullivan and other top DNC fundraisers to approach big Democratic donors who could make at least a contribution of at least $50,000 to the re-election campaign of Carey, then in a pitched battle with James Hoffa, Jr. Under McAuliffe's scheme, Sullivan testified, the Teamster's Union would later recycle that $50,000 back into various Democratic Party accounts. Once again, McAuliffe was never charged with wrongdoing and his lawyer, Richard Ben-Veniste, repeatedly said there's was nothing illegal in his client's plan. He lives a charmed life.

● ● ● ● ●

TERRY MCAULIFFE WAS BORN IN 1957 IN SYRACUSE, NEW York. His father was a longtime Democratic powerbroker in upper state New York and a top fundraiser for the party. Terry got into politics at a young age. But as anyone can tell there's not much evidence that he was ever excited about policy issues. The environment, abortion rights, civil rights, peace. These great issues didn't turn Terry on. Instead, he was entranced by the mechanics of political fundraising, party planning and schmoozing with business elites and Hollywood celebrities.

He made a beeline for the Beltway, attending Catholic University. Through his father's influence, he got a position as a fundraiser for Jimmy Carter. And then he was off and running, renting his financial services to House and senate races and gubernatorial elections.

In the meantime, McAuliffe managed to earn the obligatory law degree from Georgetown University. Then in 1984, he began to fine-tune his craft under the wing of Tony Coelho, the longtime House whip and master fundraiser from California. At the time, Coelho was heading up the Democratic Congressional

Campaign Committee, the main DNC fundraising apparatus for House races.

More than anyone, Coelho laid the foundations for the Democratic Party's open courting of big business. And Terry McAuliffe, working from the master's Rolodex, served as Coelho's chief apprentice, sprinting from one Beltway lobby shop to the next offering prime access to Democratic powerbrokers for political cash, hard and soft money, the new coin of the realm.

The young fundraiser learned an early lesson. No enterprise was off-limits, no matter how tarnished the reputation of the company: weapons-makers, oil companies, chemical manufacturers, banks, sweatshop tycoons. Indeed, McAuliffe made his mark by targeting corporations with festering problems, ranging from liability suits to environmental and worker safety restraints to bothersome federal regulators. The more desperate these enterprises were for political intervention, the more money McAuliffe knew he could seduce into DNC coffers. What about environmental groups? Big labor? The traditional core of the Democratic Party? Not only didn't their objections (assuming they voiced any) matter, they actually made McAuliffe's pitch more appealing to the corporadoes. After all, the Republicans didn't have any sway over these organizations. Triangulation, the backstabbing political playbook of Clintontime, originated as a fundraising gimmick. A very lucrative one.

In the early 90s, really big money began to pour into the DNC. McAuliffe recruited robust donations from Arco and Chevron, Entergy and Enron, Phillip Morris and Monsanto, Boeing and Lockheed, Citibank and Weyerhaeuser. Many of these corporations had all but abandoned the Democrats during the Reagan era. McAuliffe lured them back with promises of favorable treatment by a new generation of anti-regulatory Democrats attuned to the special needs of multinational corporations. This was the mulch bed from which the Clinton presidency took root.

By 1994, Clinton himself had aligned himself to McAuliffe's magic touch. He tapped him as the chief fundraiser for the 1996 reelection campaign. In this capacity, McAuliffe masterminded some of the more risqué political fundraising operations since the Kennedy era. There were the fundraisers at Buddhist temples in California. There were the notorious coffee klatches, where for a six-figure contribution to the DNC, corporate executives were brought to the White House for some face-time with Bill and Hillary, Al and Tipper, and a retinue of cabinet secretaries, with pen in hand ready to address any nagging problem. McAuliffe also devised the plan to rent out the Lincoln Bedroom to top contributors for slumber parties with the president.

Over the course of the next six years, McAuliffe was personally responsible for raising, largely from corporate sources, more than $300 million for the DNC.

●●●●●

THE SCENE: THE MCI CENTER IN WASHINGTON, D.C. THE date: May 14, 2000. The Event: "BBQ and Blue Jeans Gala." It's Terry McAuliffe's biggest party yet. A star-studded gathering of DC lobbyists, corporate executives and Hollywood liberals, all dressed in blue jeans, eating BBQ and listening to the blues and country music. It was also the single biggest fundraiser in history. More than $25 million was raised for the DNC in a single night.

Toward the end of the evening, Al Gore lumbered his way onto the stage and seized the microphone. He directed the spotlight turned on McAuliffe, the real star of the evening. "Terry", Gore said, "You are the greatest fundraiser in the history of the universe." The crowd thundered with applause for the man who had just lightened their wallets of several thousands of dollars.

Gore would soon come to rue those fervent words. While most Democrats blamed Katherine Harris or the Supreme Court for the loss of the White House to George W. Bush, McAuliffe pointed the finger at Gore. The fundraiser believed that Gore ran an inept campaign, misspending the precious millions he had worked so diligently to raise. McAuliffe detested the way that Gore distanced himself from the Clintons and refused to allow the president to campaign for him even in key southern states. Even worse from McAuliffe's perspective, Gore had subtly dissed Clinton on the campaign trail, suggesting that he himself was a man of firmer moral sinew than the embattled president.

When Gore lost, the party fell back into the control of the Clintons and their chief emissary, Terry McAuliffe. The fundraiser swiftly took his revenge out on Gore. In late January, 2001, as the moving vans where pulling away from the White House, McAuliffe planned a major send off for the Clintons at Andrews Air Base. All the top Democrats were there; many were invited to give tributes to the first couple in front of the national TV cameras. Al Gore, naturally, expected to give the keynote farewell address. But McAuliffe refused to allow Gore even near a microphone. Gore wasn't permitted to speak a single word. "McAuliffe didn't want Gore to speak", a top aide at the DNC told the *Washington Post*. "McAuliffe didn't even want Gore there. The send off was about good memories, success stories. And the VP wasn't either."

McAuliffe's implacable loyalty to Clinton was soon rewarded. Later in 2001, Bill Clinton engineered the ouster of Joe Andrew as head of the DNC and installed McAuliffe, who only months earlier had offered to purchase the Clintons a house in Chappaqua, New York for $1.3 million, as the chief of the party. As the head of the DNC, McAuliffe was now in a position to protect the Clintons' legacy, reward loyalists, punish party dissidents and select the next presidential nominee.

When Gore began to flirt with the notion of challenging Bush in 2004, McAuliffe went to work to kill off his campaign before it even started. He went straight to Gore's top political sponsors and advised them to withhold funds from the Gore campaign chest. He was tremendously persuasive, convincing even some of Gore's most loyal backers, such as financier James Tisch, to deny money to their old friend.

The sabotage of the nascent Gore 2004 campaign was just a run-up for the demolition job McAuliffe directed against the unauthorized campaign of Vermont governor Howard Dean. The Dean threat had almost nothing to do with any perceived ideological heresy from the Vermonter. After all Dean was a run-of-the-mill neoliberal who pretty much aped the centrist economic policies of Clinton. The real threat posed by Dean came from his determination to raise millions in campaign contributions outside of the precincts of the DNC. McAuliffe's control over the party stems from his role as the prime dispenser of campaign cash, the elixir necessary to keep political recipients loyal to the party leadership and its policies. Dean showed another way was possible and he had to be put down.

But after the Dean juggernaut was scuttled, McAuliffe reached out a helping hand to the defeated candidate. As usual, the hand proffered money. The Dean campaign was in debt, the legions of Deaniacs seething with rage over the demolition of their hero. McAuliffe offered to help pay off Dean's debts and set up his new institute, Democracy for America. In return, Dean worked to calm his troops, imploring them not to abandon the party for the independent campaign of Ralph Nader.

● ● ● ● ●

TERRY MCAULIFFE DIDN'T JUST USE HIS BUSINESS CONTACTS TO fatten the accounts of the Democratic National Committee; he also deftly exploited them to inflate his own fortune, which now nudges toward nine figures. A similar fruitful intimacy with corporate cronies led to Tony Coelho's stunning fall from grace, but McAuliffe never looked back. His trajectory has been decidedly prosperous and, to this point, utterly immune to the slumping fortunes of the economy outside the confines of the Beltway. These days McAuliffe says he wants to resurrect the Misery Index, but he's not acquainted with any of the numbers.

In 1996, McAuliffe met a young corporate tycoon named Gary Winnick, who had once referred to himself as the richest man in Los Angeles. Winnick ran Global Crossing, a fiber-optics company chartered in the tax-friendly haven of Bermuda. At the time McAuliffe met Winnick, Global Crossing was a privately held company, poised to cash in on the deregulation of the telecom industry and the new opportunities in China. In 1997, Winnick offered McAuliffe the opportunity to purchase $100,000 worth of Global Crossing stock.

When Global Crossing shares went public in 1998, the value of the stock soared. Operating with an acute sensitivity to the fluctuations of the market bordering on ESP, McAuliffe sold his shares at the precise moment the stock peaked. McAuliffe told the *New York Times* he pocketed $18 million in the deal. Within a few months, Global Crossing's stock collapsed, the company plunged into bankruptcy and more than a third of its workforce were tossed into the ranks of the unemployed.

McAuliffe also served as an on-call DC fixer for Winnick in those optimistic days following the Clinton reelection. In early 1997, McAuliffe set up shop in an office in downtown DC owned by a Winnick company called Pacific Capital Group. According to a boastful McAuliffe, Winnick hired him as a consultant to "help work some deals" with the federal government. "Gary was looking for some political action", McAuliffe told *Worth* magazine. "He wanted a stable of people around him with great contacts."

Few people inside the Beltway enjoyed better contacts than McAuliffe, as Winnick would soon discover. At an appearance in Los Angeles later that year, Bill Clinton lavished on Winnick his personal endorsement. "Gary Winnick has been a friend of mine for some time now and I'm thrilled by the success that Global Crossing has had."

There's no evidence that Winnick and Clinton had even met each other before that evening. But the endorsement proved fruitful. It signaled not only Clinton's faith in the company, but also sent a message to federal agencies that Global Crossing was a firm that they should do business with. It soon paid off. A few months later Global Crossing won a $400 million contract from the Pentagon after repeated prodding from the White House.

After the contract was awarded, McAuliffe arranged for Winnick to play a round of golf with Clinton. Shortly after the afternoon on the links, Winnick donated $1 million to the Clinton presidential library.

Winnick's joy was short lived, however. In the winter of 2001, the Pentagon rescinded the Global Crossing deal following an investigation by the Inspector General of the Defense Department, which raised questions over how the contract was awarded and Global Crossing's ability to fulfill its obligations. Later, the company fell into the financial death noted above.

The attack dogs in the Bush White House never really made much of McAuliffe's ripe ties to Global Crossing. Why? Global Crossing had been almost equally generous to the Bush family.

In 1997, Global Crossing invited former President George H.W. Bush to address company executives in Tokyo, Japan. At the time, Bush's standard speaking fee was $80,000. The morning after the speech, Bush had breakfast with Winnick. Winnick advised Bush that it would prove much more profitable for the former president to accept payment in Global Crossing stock, then privately held, than cash. Bush agreed. Soon the company went public and the value of Bush's stock swelled to more than $14 million. Not a bad pay-off for an hour's speech. To complete the symmetry, one of Winnick's top executives also serves as a trustee of the G.H.W. Bush Presidential Library Fund.

Winnick tried to cover all of his bases. Yet as with Enron and Tyco, even the most judicious dispensation of money across the political spectrum couldn't save a company that had been looted from the inside out. Global Crossing went down and so did Winnick. But the politicians who made it all possible remain indemnified from any liability for the carnage, protected by a mutually advantageous non-aggression pact.

Never bite the hands that feed the system.

Chapter 16

"To speak of Karl Rove's successes is to speak of the failures and corruptions of American politics and public life."

Steve Perry
Rove: the Manager and the Playing Field

Rove: the Manager and the Playing Field

KARL ROVE HAS BEEN A REMARKABLY UNCHANGING COM-modity. Since childhood, politics and the Republican Party have been his sole concerns. (Asked a few years ago when he first started weighing a presidential campaign, he named the day he was born, December 25, 1950.) And his entire career, spanning some 30 years, is bound together in large measure by his professional ties and personal devotion to George Bush the father and George Bush the son.

Which is to say, Rove is not quite the puppet master that the Bush-is-stupid crowd supposes. The history of his relationship with W is fraught with tensions, contests of ego and will, and occasional political disagreements that Rove did not always win. One token of the ambivalent undercurrent between them is the invariably withering series of nicknames Bush has applied to Rove: Boy Genius, Mr. Big Shot, Turd Blossom. (In west Texas, you see, desert flowers sometimes sprout from cow manure.) Rove may be the man with big ideas, but he is also, like everyone else around W, a subordinate - at best, an honorary member of the Bush clan.

You don't have to be a psychohistorian to see in it an element of compensation. Rove's family life as a child sounds fairly dismal. His father, a mineral geologist, was gone from home for long stretches, and finally walked out for good on Christmas Eve, 1969, which was also the eve of Karl's 19th birthday. A few years earlier, the family had uprooted from Nevada to move to Salt Lake City just as Karl was entering high school. According to *Bush's Brain*, Wayne Slater and James Moore's biography, the whole experience left Rove hungering for images of perma-nence, legitimacy and authority. "In a city where the prevalent influences were political and religious," they wrote, "his family was neither. He grew up in an apolitical household, without religious mooring. Friend Mark Dangerfield told a reporter that it seemed to bother Rove that 'he was raised in a completely nonreligious home.'" (Though Rove may never have caught the religion bug himself, it figured prominently from the start in Rove's service to his one true god, the Republican Party.)

Rove's ties to Bush the Elder commenced in 1973, when the latter was the Republican national chairman and Karl aspired to be the president of the College Republicans. It was a post Rove could not win by the numbers. To circumvent them, he claimed that the organization was not adhering procedurally to the College Republican charter, and mounted credentials challenges to supporters of his opponent, Robert Edgeworth. In the end Rove essentially declared himself the winner of a separate election. The controversy got kicked upstairs to Bush, who awarded the election to Rove.

Later, in retaliation, Edgeworth leaked to the *Washington Post* that Rove was teaching dirty tricks seminars to young Republicans – and fresh off the humiliation of Watergate, no less. Bush promptly excommunicated Edgeworth from the Republican Party for his disloyalty in leaking the story. Rove, along with his friend and College Republicans ally Lee Atwater, became favored Bush protégés. Rove moved to Texas in 1977 to toil as a fundraiser on George Sr.'s failed presidential exploration PAC, the Fund for Limited Government. A year later he worked on an unsuccessful primary run for the Texas legislature by George W.

If his efforts on behalf of the Bushes didn't come to much at first, Rove's own career took off in Texas, where he would engineer a complete Republican takeover of the state's elective offices in a little over a decade's time. After working for a while as Governor Bill Clements's chief of staff, he started his own business in 1981: Karl Rove & Co., direct-mail specialists.

Nicholas Lemann's May 2003 *New Yorker* profile of Rove is one of the few sketches of his career to appreciate the significance of this move:

> That Rove got his start in the direct-mail business, a technical and unglamorous political subspecialty, is important in understanding the way he thinks and operates today.... Media consultants tend to think of raising money as somebody else's job, but direct-mail consultants are fundraisers – there's that little envelope in each letter – and are more closely attuned to where the money is. Most important, direct mail consultants are in the business of narrowcasting rather than broadcasting. They have to be on perpetual patrol for new groups with intense opinions about politics.

In politics there is nothing more useful than knowing where the money is, but Rove knew more than that. A voracious student of electoral history – and one of those people possessed of a seemingly eidetic memory for numbers and statistics that bordered on the freakish – Rove always knew where the votes were, too, and could, if you cared to listen, parse them in a dozen different ways on the spot and tell you how to woo each sub-segment of voters. Yet he wasn't just a numbers geek. As Rove made the transition from producing direct mail to running political campaigns, he proved quite good at concocting sturdy, simple campaign themes for general consumption. Rove could broadcast as well as narrowcast; he had the makings of a fine minister of propaganda – the intuitive facility for adducing that single, simple idea that would win the most people to your side, and the force of personality to repeat it over and over even if it was absurd.

And he was ruthless in chasing his goals, especially when it came to rivalries or power struggles with his own Republican cohorts. One of his foes, Tom Pauken – a Christian conservative who, as state party chair of Texas Republicans, stood in Rove's way for a time – characterized him this way in *Bush's Brain*: "Lee [Atwater] was the kind of guy who'd say, hey, you were against us here but you can be for us the next time. Karl is very different. If you cross him, you're on the list. And the more you cross him over a period of time, the higher you go on the list."

A Texas Medical Association lobbyist was more terse: "It is in Karl's nature to engulf and devour and control and to rule." Rove's tendency to make every fight personal, and to the death, may yet undo him. (Remember that he and his staff are still parties to an active criminal investigation over the leak of Valerie Plame's identity.) But Rove's rage for control is inseparable from the qualities that make him excel at what he does.

In outlook, one word seems to sum up Rove best: interloper. As a non-Mormon in Utah, a nondescript middle-class kid who identified with political royalty, and more generally a conservative throughout the tumultuous 1960s, Rove defined himself repeatedly as one *a rebours*, against the grain, though a less Huysmanesque figure can scarcely be imagined. He seems to have learned two things in the process: what it feels like to count yourself part of a besieged but noble minority (which may be one reason Rove and the Republicans have been so good at crafting folksy, anti-elitist images on behalf of GOP elites), and how to rise up above any crowd and turn its attention to you.

Regarding the latter, it should be noted that geeky gentile Karl won the presidency of his largely Mormon high school class before he was through. In so doing, he must have seen the lesson that would shape his future, and punch his ticket out of Salt Lake City for good: you do not have to play by the rules, or respect the prevailing order of things, if you do your homework right, do the little things thoroughly, and – most important – act with absolute audacity when the time is right. This was quite literally how he came to the head of the College Republican class, and therefore to the attention of GHWB. (Later Rove found a Napoleon quotation that summed up his philosophy: "The whole art of war consists in a well-reasoned and extremely circumspect defensive strategy, followed by rapid and audacious attack.") Finally, it was no doubt a great boon to Rove to hone his craft in Texas, a setting where few pretended to stand on rules or balk at cronyism, and many openly admired his kind of zeal and inventiveness in the screwing of enemies.

Along the way, Rove kept up his ties to the Bush family, working on Sr.'s successful run for president in 1988. When it came time to launch the political career of George W., every pol in Texas knew that Rove – if not, necessarily, Bush – had one eye on the White House from the start. But not even Mr. Timing himself could have anticipated how ripe the world inside the Beltway would be for his style of politics by the time he arrived.

Rove is never without detailed attack strategies, but he always keeps the master plan simple. He once summed up the entire Bush 2000 campaign thus: character, not issues; and play on the other guy's turf (that is, target and take away a few Democratic strongholds, as Republicans did in West Virginia and Al Gore's home state of Tennessee). The plan for 2004 is not hard to infer. Where issues are concerned, say that tax cuts stimulate growth and the president is tough on terrorism. But once again, make the main issue character – which really means personality. Make Bush look steady, likeable, strong. Make Kerry look feckless, self-serving, cynical. Include in the mix some tough-but-sentimental ad spots that function more or less like video yule logs burning in the electronic hearth: they encourage comfort with Bush. And raise enough cash to outspend God if it comes to that.

NOW EVERY SCHOOL CHILD KNOWS THAT MODERN POLITICAL campaigns revolve around cash, but that does not begin to express the Zen of Money as Rove practices it. His famous historical obsession with the election of 1896 holds some clues. The victory of Republican William McKinley over the free-silver Democrat William Jennings Bryan represented the first time that a candidate had been packaged so much like a product, or marketed to so many discrete corners of the populace. The Republicans' success in targeting the new urban immigrant working class helped them prevail, but at unprecedented cost. To finance it, the architects of McKinley's campaign, Mark Hanna and Charles Dawes, raised the unheard-of sum of $3.5 million by direct and urgent appeal to the captains of industry.

Rove's first rule of politics is to know where the money is. His first rule of governance is to keep one's political base mollified while setting about the serious work of assuring the commanding allegiance of big political donors in the next election cycle.

It's said one quality that sets Rove apart is his ability to see the whole playing field in politics. So let's talk about the playing field that Rove seems to see.

Start with the people: they are tired, overworked, and scared – about their own livelihoods and threats from without. More important, they are woefully ignorant, and easily worn down, concerning the details of any political subject. They are acclimated to political races in which the main differences revolve around personality, and comfortable making almost entirely emotional decisions about candidates. This is an overgeneralization, but to date a viable one. Presidential elections are mass-culture phenomena, and the majority of voters in any election know very little of substance about the candidates or issues involved.

The media: on a mass basis, the medium that matters most by far is television. According to a 2003 Pew Research Center study, over 80 percent of Americans claim to get most of their news from TV. And if you take the further step of looking at TV news viewership numbers, you will find them pretty underwhelming. The only sensible conclusion is that a great many Americans consume political news in sporadic, sidelong fashion, if at all. Many others try to follow events, but lack the time for anything but a few minutes of cable news and glance at their newspaper's front page.

Two things follow. First, the relative impact of political ads versus news coverage is much greater than a casual observer might think. Second, and more important, if you can keep bad news off the front page and off TV news, most people will never even know it happened. There are only a handful of media organizations in charge of what Americans see on the national TV news, and they are always looking over their shoulders at each other. They're not just pack animals; they're a small and mostly manageable pack.

The political opposition: Please. They were pathetic to start with, and September 11 paralyzed them completely. The Democrats have been chasing Republicans since Reagan. For the past generation they have not disagreed with the GOP in principle on any of the important points of empire, capital's prerogatives, or economic austerity at home; they just fuss more and go slower. To them, elections have been battles over market share more than the direction of things. In the process, the Democratic Party has gone soft. It's politically unserious, no longer capable of putting up a sustained fight. This is nothing new. Republicans got away with Iran/contra in the 80s, and Bill Clinton was nearly booted from office for office blowjobs. George Bush I got scant flack for pardoning Iran/contra conspirators on his way out of office; Bill Clinton let a crooked financier named Marc Rich off the hook, and Republicans kept the issue in play for weeks.

All of which brings us to Karl Rove's radical insight, his claim to true genius, if he has one. He arrived in Washington knowing that the vaunted institutions of democracy were bankrupt, that the whole civics-class edifice of checks and balances, reasoned political debate, and a vigorous, impartial press amounted to a paper line you could just walk through. (The terms of his boss's 2000 win proved that: whatever might be said about fraud and chicanery in Florida, no one can dispute that it all came down to a 5-4 Supreme Court vote in which two of the justices who voted for Bush had family members who worked for his campaign.) If it wasn't quite as simple as that formulation makes it sound, the project proved no less feasible in the end. It involved the two central virtues invoked by Napoleon: audacity and an "extremely circumspect defensive strategy." For Bush/Rove in 2004, the latter means a massive effort to divert attention from the facts of Bush's record.

But the totality of their successes can't be put down to running slick campaigns. For a good three years, the Bush gang had its way with "the political process" without being called to account for much of anything. The autocratic prerogative they've enjoyed is so glaring that a line of apologetics has already been constructed for posterity: the whole political system rolled over for Bush because it was the patriotic thing to do after 9/11.

Aside from being largely untrue, this explanation also fails to explain anything. If the post-September 11 world was suddenly defined by a war against terrorism, then surely any great, or halfway-sound, democracy would have indulged in vigorous debate over the course of the fight. Voices surely would have risen up to question the wisdom of invading a nation whose terrorism threat looked – and turned out to be – fictitious. All the while, a free press would have dug in its heels and sought to illuminate the underlying issues (the range of them, mind you, not just the officially sanctioned ones) to a concerned citizenry. But none of this ever happened, unless you count the lonely, stately protests of Robert Byrd as an "opposition".

So there you go. To speak of Karl Rove's successes is to speak of the failures and corruptions of American politics and public life. They are two expressions of the same thing. Since January and the start of the Democratic presidential campaign, there has been some hint of life in the loyal opposition and the press; American newspapers have turned notably more critical in their Bush coverage. Any one of numerous potential scandals still might return to haunt the administration. There are also signs that Democrats aren't the only ones in the Washington political establishment feeling anxious about Bush's brazenness and his reckless, sloppy management of economy and empire. This circle is not a great power in electoral politics, but they could lend fuel to a media feeding frenzy, if one arose.

The president could lose this election, as I'm guessing Rove surmised early on. In crafting a campaign that is half poison-pen note, half Hallmark card, he and George W. are wagering against a lot of things: real, and serious, competition from John Kerry and the Democrats. Sustained criticism of Bush in the media. These aren't bad bets.

John Kerry has been slowly dematerializing in the public imagination since his wrap-up of the nomination came into view. He has made some trenchant criticisms of Bush, but he hasn't made any of them stick. He doesn't know how. It's still possible that Kerry and the Democrats could put the White House back on the defensive, force them off their game.

No matter how well you do political campaigns, there is always the faint chance that too many people will already have seen through you. On the other hand, Karl Rove has never lost a race yet by underestimating the integrity and rationality of American electoral politics.

Chapter 17

"The three biggest oil and gas bonanzas attributed to the rapacity of the Bush regime – the Alaska petroleum reserve, the Gulf of Mexico, and the Powder River Basin – were all initiated by the Clinton administration. Enron? Kerry's energy man was one of Enron's biggest promoters."

Jeffrey St. Clair
Oil for One and One for Oil

JEFFREY ST. CLAIR
Oil for One and One for Oil

SHORTLY AFTER JOHN KERRY SEWED UP THE DELEGATES needed to seize the Democratic nomination for president, he huddled for two hours with James Hoffa, Jr., the boss of the Teamsters Union. The topic was oil. The Teamsters wanted more of it at cheaper prices. They had suspicions about Kerry. After all, the senator had already won the backing of the Sierra Club, who touted him as the most environmentally enlightened member of the US Senate.

Hoffa emerged from the meeting sporting a shark-like grin. Hoffa and the Teamsters have long pushed for opening up the Arctic National Wildlife Refuge (ANWR) to drilling and for the construction of a natural gas pipcline to cut across some of the wildest land in North America from the tundra of Alaska to Chicago. "Kerry says, look, I am against drilling in ANWR, but I am going to put that pipeline in, and we're going to drill like never before", Hoffa reported. "They are going to drill all over, according to him. And he says, we're going to be drilling all over the United States". Kerry didn't stop to comment. He slipped out the door and into a waiting SUV.

The Bush administration has been aptly pegged as a petroarchy. It isn't so much under the sway of Big Oil as it is infested top to bottom with oil operatives, starting with the president and vice president. Eight cabinet members and the National Security Advisor directly from executive jobs in the oil industry, as did 32 other Bush-appointed officials in the Office of Management and Budget, Pentagon, State Department, and the departments of Energy, Agriculture and, most crucially in terms of opening up what remains of the American wilderness to the drillers, Interior.

The point man in the Bush's administration's oil raid on the public estate is Stephen J. Griles, Gale Norton's top lieutenant at the Interior Department. As Deputy Secretary of Interior, Griles is the man who holds the keys to the nation's oil and mineral reserves. Since landing this prized position, he used those keys to unlock nearly every legal barrier to exploitation, opening the public lands to a carnival of corporate plunder. He became the toast of Texas.

From the time he took his oath of office, Griles was a congressional investigation waiting to happen. The former coal industry flack was one of Bush's most outrageous appointments, an arrogant booster of the very energy cartel he was meant to regulate. His track record could not be given even the slightest green gloss. A veteran of the Reagan administration, Griles schemed closely with disgraced Interior Secretary James Watt to open the public lands of the West to unfettered access by oil and mining companies, many of whom funded Watt's strange outpost of divinely inspired environmental exploitation, the Mountain States Legal Center.

As Deputy Director of Surface Mining, Griles gutted strip-mining regulations and was a relentless booster of the oil-shale scheme, one of the most outlandish giveaways and environmental blunders of the last century. He also pushed to overturn the popular moratorium on off shore oil drilling on the Pacific Coast, a move of such extreme zealotry in the service of big oil that it even caught Reagan off guard.

After leaving public office, Griles quickly cashed in on his iniquitous tenure in government by launching a DC lobbying firm called J. Stephen Griles and Associates. He soon drummed up a list of clients including Arch Coal, the American Gas Association, National Mining Association, Occidental Petroleum, Pittston Coal and more than 40 other gas, mining and energy concerns, big and small, foreign and domestic.

Then Griles was picked as Norton's chief deputy. After contentious senate hearings that exposed his various and lucrative entanglements with the oil and gas industry, Griles was finally confirmed to office on July 7, 2001. He later signed two separate statements agreeing to recuse himself from direct involvement any Interior Department matters that might involve his former clients. He later flouted both of those agreements, as disclosed by his own calendar of meetings, liberated through a Freedom of Information Act filing made by Friends of the Earth.

As the calendar and meeting notes reveal, Griles used the cover of the 9/11 attacks and the war on Iraq to advance his looting of the public domain for the benefit of some of his former clients and business cronies. He pushed rollbacks in environmental standards for air and water; advocated increased oil and gas drilling on public lands; tried to exempt the oil industry from royalty payments; and sought to create new loopholes in regulations governing strip mining.

Griles wasted no time compiling a wish list for his pals. Within days of assuming office, Griles convened a series of parleys between his former clients and Interior Department officials to chart a game plan for accelerating mining, oil leasing and coal-methane extraction from public lands. Between August of 2001 and January of this year, Griles met at least 7 times with former clients; 15 times with companies represented by his former client the National Mining Association; on at least 16 occasions he arranged meetings between himself, former clients, and other administration officials to discuss rollback of air pollution standards for power plants, oil refineries and industrial boilers; on 12 occasions he arranged similar meetings between regulators and former clients regarding coal mining.

Griles was an ownership partner in a DC lobbying firm called National Environmental Strategies, a polluter's lobby founded in 1990 by Marc Himmelstein and Haley Barbour. Barbour soon left the firm to become head of the Republican National Committee. Griles moved in.

When he was nominated as deputy secretary of Interior, Griles was forced to sell his interest in the firm for $1.1 million, and he fixed up a deal with Himmelstein, a friend and Republican powerbroker. Instead of paying Griles off in a lump sum, Himmelstein promised to pay the Bush official $284,000 each year over the next four years. Griles claimed he arranged this kind of payment plan so as not to leave NES "strapped for cash".

But in effect Griles remained financially tied to the health of Himmelstein's firm. And, in fact, Himmelstein admitted that over the past two years he and Griles have gotten together several times over beers and dinner.

As these pungent episodes from Grile's tenure at Interior revealed, the Bush administration's fatal flaw has been its inclination to over-reach, such as when the Interior Department, at the prodding of politically tone-deaf Dick Cheney, unveiled a plan to offer oil leases off the coast of Florida. The president's brother, Jeb, shot the plan down. A similar blunder occurred in California, where new offshore leasing had been banned since the oil spills of the 1970s. The Bush administration floated a plan for new leases off the coast of Northern California, Oregon and Washington. They backed down after the scheme met with resistance from the likes of Arnold Schwarzenegger. Still these should be viewed as probing raids, testing the tenacity of the opposition, while the real opportunities for plunder were being pursued in more compliant terrain, where the door had already been opened by the Clinton administration.

● ● ● ● ●

BUT JIMMY HOFFA WAS ON TO SOMETHING. DESPITE WHAT YOU hear from the Sierra Club, Kerry and his Democratic cohorts have never aligned themselves in opposition to the interests of the oil cartels. Far from it. In Clintontime, oil industry lobbyists flowed through the White House as easily as crude through the Alaskan pipeline, leaving behind campaign loot and wish lists. Several oil execs even enjoyed sleepovers in the Lincoln bedroom. Hazel O'Leary, Clinton's first Energy Secretary, traveled the world with oil execs in tow, brokering deals from India to China. Meanwhile, Ms. O'Leary, a former utility executive from Minnesota, compiled an enemies list of environmentalists and reporters who raised unsettling questions about her cozy ties to big oil.

In the summer of 1994, while Clinton vacationed in the Tetons, just down the trout stream from Dick Cheney's ranch, eight top oil executives dropped in for a visit. This confab in Jackson Hole became Clinton's version of the Cheney energy task force. The oil moguls pressed Clinton for a number of concessions: 1. Increased drilling on the Outer Continental Shelf, especially in the Gulf of Mexico; 2. A break on royalty payments; 3. Expedited leasing for coal-bed methane the Rocky Mountain Front; 4. Opening the National Petroleum Reserve-Alaska to drilling; 5. Removal of the ban on export of Alaskan crude oil to overseas refineries.

At 24 million acres in size, the National Petroleum Reserve-Alaska stood as the largest undeveloped tract of land in North America. Located on the Arctic plain just west of Prudhoe Bay, it is almost indistinguishable ecologically from the hallowed grounds of ANWR, which abuts the eastern edge of big oil's industrial city on the tundra. The same ecology, only much bigger. The oil industry had craved entry into the NPR-A since the 1920s, when it was set aside for entry only in the case of a national emergency. Clinton and his Interior Secretary Bruce Babbitt gave them what Nixon, Ford, Reagan and Bush had been unable or unwilling to deliver.

But there's more. For 25 years, the oil companies operating on the North Slope had been required to refine the crude oil in the United States. Indeed, the opening of the North Slope to oil drilling, and the construction of the leaky 820-mile long Trans-Alaska Pipeline to transport the crude from Prudhoe Bay to Valdez, was sanctioned by the US Congress only because the oil was intended to buttress America's energy independence. Exports of raw crude were explicitly banned. At the time Senator Walter Mondale warned that the oil companies would eventually have the ban overturned, saying they had always intended it to be the "Trans-Alaska-Japan pipeline". Mondale correctly foresaw that the oil companies would export large shipments of the Alaskan crude to Asia in order to keep winter heating fuel prices high in the Midwestern states. Now, nearly three decades after this prediction, the oil companies have the jackpot in their grasp.

The winning strategy to lift the export ban was hatched by Tommy Boggs, the Rasputin of American lobbyists, whose firm, Patton, Boggs, represents a thick portfolio of oil companies, including Exxon, Mobil, Shell, and Ashland. In this instance, Boggs was the advance man for Alyeska, owned by the Alaskan oil consortium. Alyeska operates the Trans-Alaska pipeline and supervises oil extraction on the North Slope. Alyeska is owned by the consortium of companies doing business in northern Alaska. In an August 1995 memo to a prospective client, Boggs, a golfing pal of Bill Clinton, boasts of his bipartisan expertise in moving the measure through Congress: "We have a very good working relationship with the Alaska delegation, having led the private-sector effort to get exports of Alaskan North Slope oil approved by the 104th Congress and signed by President Clinton". Boggs' normal price tag is a robust $550 per hour, which translates into $22,000 for a 40-hour week.

Students of the political economy of the Clinton White House are correct in assuming that the billions handed over by

Clinton to the Alaskan oil cartel were predicated on a substantial river of slush coming the other way. The fund-raisers at 1600 Pennsylvania Avenue were not disappointed.

After all, ARCO – the prime beneficiary of the new Alaskan oil bonanza – is one of the preeminent sponsors of the American political system. The oil giant maintains a hefty federal political action committee. In the 1996 election cycle, the ARCO PAC handed out more than $357,000. But this is only the beginning. Over the same period, ARCO pumped $1.25 million of soft money into the tanks of the Republican and Democratic national committees. The company contributed at least another $500,000 in state elections, where corporations can often give directly to candidates.

At the time, Robert Healy was ARCO's vice-president for governmental affairs. On October 25, 1995, Healy attended a White House coffee "klatsch" with Vice President Al Gore and Marvin Rosen, finance chairman of the Democratic National Committee. A few days before the session, Healy himself contributed $1,000 to the Clinton/Gore re-election campaign. But from July through December of 1995, largely under Healy's direction, ARCO poured $125,000 into the coffers of the DNC.

The man who did much of ARCO's political dirty work in Washington, D.C. was Charles T. Manatt, former chairman of the Democratic Party. Manatt runs a high-octane lobbying shop called Manatt, Phelps, Rothenberg and Evans, formerly the lair of Mickey Kantor. The lobbyist attended a White House coffee with Clinton on May 26, 1995. In 1995 and 1996, Manatt alone doled out $117,150 in hard and soft money. Members of Manatt's family threw in $7,000. His law firm kicked in $22,500 and the firm's PAC another $81,109.

Inside the Clinton cabinet, Manatt's former partner, Kantor, became the most strident agitator for lifting the export ban on Alaskan oil, promoting it as a vital prong in the administration's Asian trade policy. Kantor resigned his position as Secretary of

Commerce and resumed his law practice with the Manatt, Phelps firm.

ARCO's former CEO, Lodwrick Cook, is a personal friend of Bill Clinton. In 1994, Cook celebrated his birthday at the White House. The President himself presented the oil executive with a towering cake. Cook traveled with Commerce Secretary Ron Brown on a trade junket to China in August 1994. During that trip, Cook and Brown negotiated ARCO's investment in the huge Zhenhai refinery outside Shanghai. The refinery is now ready to process Alaskan crude, which suggests that at least two years before Clinton's executive order on oil exports in the spring of 1996, ARCO had inside knowledge of what was to come.

In one of the more pungent hypocrisies of the Clinton age, the green establishment largely went along with Babbitt's plan to open the petroleum reserve, under the deluded impression that to do so meant they would be able to keep the oil companies out of ANWR.

Of course, by swallowing Babbitt's plan to open the petroleum reserve to oil drilling the greens basically undermined nearly every ecological and cultural argument for keeping the drillers out of ANWR.

Like ANWR, the petroleum reserve is home to a caribou herd. But the Western Arctic caribou herd that migrates across the reserve is almost twice as large as the herd that travels across ANWR. Similarly, the petroleum reserve is home to a slate of declining species, including polar bears, Arctic wolves and foxes, and musk ox.

Unlike ANWR, the petroleum reserve contains one of the great rivers of the Arctic, the Colville River, the largest on the North Slope, which starts high in the Brooks Range and curves for 300 miles through the heart of the reserve to a broad delta on the Arctic Ocean near the Inupiat village of Nuiqsut.

The Colville River canyon and the nearby lakes and marshes form one of the world's most important migratory bird staging areas. Over 20 percent of the entire population of Pacific black brant molt each year at Teshekpuk Lake alone. The bluffs along the Colville River are recognized as the most prolific raptor breeding grounds in the Arctic, providing critical habitat for the peregrine falcon and rough-legged hawk.

In early 2003, the Bush administration moved to expand the drilling in the NPR-A, originally approved by Babbitt and Clinton. Under the Bush plan, 9 million acres would be opened to drilling almost immediately and another 3 million acres, near the Inupiat village of Wainwright, would be opened later in the decade. The plan, tailored to meet the needs of ConocoPhillips, will call for thousands of wells, hundreds of miles of road, dozens of waste dumps and a network of pipelines to transport the oil to Prudhoe Bay and the trans-Alaska pipeline.

But oil and gas may not be the only prize. The BLM, which never misses an opportunity to pursue maximum development of public lands, estimates that the petroleum reserve may harbor approximately 40 percent of all coal remaining in the US (400 billion to 4 trillion US tons).

●●●●●

WHEN HOFFA VOWED THAT KERRY WAS GOING TO DRILL EVERY-where except ANWR like never before, he was talking about the NPR-A. He was also referring to plans to sink oil wells into the Kenai Peninsula and off of Kodiak Island and near the Chugach forest. There are also more than 670 lease applications piled up in the Clinton years for new offshore oil development in Alaska, from the Gulf of Alaska, to the Copper River Delta (perhaps the greatest remaining salmon fishery in the world), to Cook Inlet (flanked by the Katmai National Park and the Kenai Peninsula) to Bristol Bay, to the Chukchi Sea up by Point Hope, to the Beaufort Sea. In other words, under both the Kerry and Bush energy plans the entire coast of Alaska is now in play.

And not only Alaska.

The biggest oil rush in recent American history is taking place not on the North Slope, where reserves are ebbing out, but on the Great Plains, at the foot of the Rocky Mountains, in Montana and Wyoming. Here are huge deposits of coal methane clustered in Power River Basin in Montana and Wyoming. These reserves are worth billions of dollars and long craved by the natural gas industry. This looms as the largest energy development project in the country and has been assailed by environmentalists and native groups as an environmental nightmare.

The project, which calls for the development of more than 80,000 coal-methane wells, is so fraught with danger that even the Bush administration's own EPA issued a report sharply criticizing the environmental consequences of the scheme. Among the findings:

> the 80,000 coal methane wells will discharge nearly 20,000 gallons of salty water each day onto the ground surface, fouling the land, creeks and aquatic life; over its life span, the project will deplete the underground aquifer of more than 4 trillion gallons of water that will take hundreds of years to replenish; full-scale production will also entail 17,000 miles of new roads, 20,000 miles of pipelines and will turn nearly 200,000 acres of rangeland into an industrial zone.

This rare rebuke from the normally supine EPA roused Steven Griles into furious action. On April 12, 2002, Griles sent a scorching memo under his Department of Interior letterhead chastising the EPA for dragging its feet on the project. He chided the agency of being uncooperative with industry. It turns out that Griles had formerly represented the very companies that he was now accusing the EPA of failing to give proper deference to. As a lobbyist, Griles's clients included the Coal Bed Methane Ad Hoc Committee, Devon Energy, Redstone and Western Gas Resources, all companies seeking to gain access to the Powder River Basin gas fields. His old firm, NES, also hosted an industry-sponsored tour of Powder River Basin for EPA and Interior Department officials. NES also represents Griles' former client Devon Energy, which stands to make a killing if the deal is approved.

Griles's meddling in this matter came to the attention of the Department's lawyers. On May 8, they forced Griles to sign an agreement disqualifying himself from any further involvement in the coal-methane issue. He later said he did so "for all the world to know that I'm not even going to be talking to anybody about it again".

Griles has been rightfully vilified for his role in the Powder River Basin scandal, which prompted investigations by the Justice Department, Congress and the Inspectors General Office at the Interior Department. But none of this started under Bush. Not Alaska, not the Gulf of Mexico, not the Powder River Basin.

Here's David Hayes, Undersecretary of Interior for Energy, testifying before Congress in July of 2000 on the Clinton legacy for oil leasing on public lands and offshore sites. "The Clinton Administration is supportive of the U.S. domestic oil and gas industry", Hayes told the Senate Committee on Energy and Natural Resources. "We have supported efforts to increase oil and natural gas recovery in the deep waters of the Gulf of Mexico; we have conducted a number of extremely successful, environmentally sound off-shore oil and gas lease sales; and we have opened a portion of the National Petroleum Reserve-Alaska (NPR-A) to environmentally responsible oil and gas development, where an estimated 10 trillion cubic feet (tcf) of recoverable natural gas resources lie in the northeast section of the reserve".

Hayes boasted that while domestic oil production had declined on private lands since 1989, the Clinton administration responded by boosting oil production on public lands. Under Clinton oil production from public lands increased by more than 13 percent from 1992 figures under Bush the first, widely decried by liberals as being owned by big oil. Here are the numbers cited by Hayes for BLM oil leasing under Clinton. He called the figures impressive, which they are, although sobering might have been a more precise description:

- leasing in the Gulf of Mexico to increase almost tenfold between 1992 and 1997.
- From 1993 to 1999, 6,538 new leases were issued covering approximately 35 million acres of the Outer Continental Shelf.
- Lease Sale 175 in the Central Gulf of Mexico, held on March 15, 2000, offered 4,203 blocks (22.29 million acres) for lease. We received 469 bids on 344 blocks. 334 leases were awarded.
- More than 40 million acres of Federal OCS are currently under lease. Approximately 94% of the existing OCS leases (7,900) are in the Gulf, and about 1,500 of these leases are producing.
- Issued over 28,000 leases and approved over 15,000 permits to drill.
- In 1999, the BLM held a lease sale offering 425 tracts on 3.9 million acres in the National Petroleum Reserve-Alaska.
- Implemented legislation changing the competitive lease term from 5 years to 10 years, allowing lessees greater flexibility in exploration without endangering the lease.
- Oversaw a 60 percent increase in the production of natural gas on Federal onshore lands over the past 7 years – from 1.3 trillion cubic feet in 1992 to 2.0 trillion cubic feet in 1999.

Here's Hayes speaking reverently about the Powder River Basin coal bed methane leases, which liberals and greens have tried to lay solely at the feet of Bush and Griles: "Estimates of recoverable gas reserves on public lands from this basin alone are as high as 9 trillion cubic feet. If maximum operating capacity of the current pipelines in the Powder River Basin is achieved, production could be as much as 1 billion cubic feet per day. That will produce enough fuel to heat nearly fifty thousand homes in the United States for twenty years. Industry is producing the gas and submitting applications for permits to drill at an unprecedented rate and, presently, there are more than 4,000 coal bed methane wells in the basin. Upon completion of further environmental analysis, we expect to nearly double that amount."

The only real difference between the Clinton plan for the Powder River Basin and the Bush scheme is that the Bush administration, prodded by Steven Griles, moved to accelerate the leasing planned by Clinton, Babbitt and Hayes and truncate the environmental reviews. The end result was a foregone conclusion under both administrations.

So, the three biggest oil and gas bonanzas attributed to the rapacity of the Bush regime – the Alaska petroleum reserve, the Gulf of Mexico, and the Powder River Basin – were all initiated by the Clinton administration.

One more note on David Hayes. Before joining the Clinton team, Hayes served as the chairman of the Environmental Law Institute, a DC green group. But this was only a part-time position. His day job was as a lawyer/lobbyist at the powerhouse DC firm of Latham and Watkins, which represents a plump roster of corporations seeking to plunder the very lands as deputy secretary of Interior he would be charged with protecting. After leaving the Clinton administration, Hayes navigated a soft-landing back to his old spot at Latham and Watkins. How is this any different from the lucrative migrations of the hated Steven Griles, who traveled from the Reagan administration to an oil lobby shop to the Bush II administration? The revolving door waits for no one.

● ● ● ● ●

WHEN IT COMES TO OIL POLICY BUSH RELIES ON GRILES, WHILE John Kerry turns to Ralph Cavanagh, the top energy guru at the Natural Resources Defense Council, the neo-liberal environmental group headed by John Adams. In Clintontime, Adams and his group made a notorious splash when they publicly betrayed their fellow environmentalists by endorsing NAFTA, the trade pact with Mexico hotly opposed by a tender coalition of labor and greens. NRDC's endorsement shattered the coalition and secured passage of the bill through congress, a prize that had been denied the first Bush administration. Adams felt no regrets. He later gloated about "breaking the back of the environmental opposition to NAFTA".

Ralph Cavanagh is exceptionally close to John Kerry and his wife, Teresa Heinz. In fact, Heinz's foundation bestowed on Cavanagh its annual eco-genius award and a $250,000 check for his pioneering work in energy policy. But just what did this work entail?

Well, while his boss John Adams pushed free trade, Ralph Cavanagh hawked the deregulation of the energy business in the name of environmental efficiency, an old canard discredited in the progressive era. Cavanagh plays the role of Betty Crocker in bestowing green seals of approval for enviro-conscience and selfless devotion to the public weal by corporations like, well, Enron.

These green seals of approval were part of the neoliberal pitch, that fuddy-duddy regulation should yield to modern, "market-oriented solutions" to environmental problems, which essentially means bribing corporations in the hope they'll stop their polluting malpractices. Indeed, NRDC and EDF were always the prime salesfolk of neoliberal remedies for environmental problems. In fact, NRDC was socked into the Enron lobby machine so deep you couldn't see the soles of its feet. Here's what happened.

In 1997 high-flying Enron found itself in a pitched battle in Oregon, where it planned to acquire Portland General Electric, Oregon's largest public utility. Warning that Enron's motives were of a highly predatory nature, the staff of the state's Public Utility Commission (PUC) opposed the merger. They warned that an Enron takeover would mean less ability to protect the environment, increased insecurity for PGE's workers and, in all likelihood, soaring prices. Other critics argued that Enron's actual plan was to cannibalize PGE, in particular its hydropower, which Enron would sell into California's energy market.

But at the very moment when such protests threatened to balk Enron of its prize, into town rode Ralph Cavanagh. Cavanagh lost no time whipping the refractory Oregon greens into line. In concert with Enron, the NRDC man put together a memo of understanding, pledging that the company would lend financial support to some of these groups' pet projects.

But Cavanagh still had some arduous politicking ahead. An OK for the merger had to come from the PUC, whose staff was adamantly opposed. So, on Valentine's Day, 1997, Cavanagh showed up at a hearing in Salem, Oregon, to plead Enron's case.

Addressing the three PUC commissioners, Cavanagh averred that this was "the first time I've ever spoken in support of a utility merger". If so, it was the quickest transition from virginity to seasoned service in the history of intellectual prostitution. Cavanagh flaunted the delights of an Enron embrace: "What we've put before you with this company is, we believe, a robust assortment of public benefits for the citizens of Oregon which would not emerge, Mr. Chairman, without the merger".

With a warble in his throat, Cavanagh moved into rhetorical high gear: "'Can you trust Enron? On stewardship issues and public benefit issues I've dealt with this company for a decade, often in the most contentious circumstances, and the answer is, yes".

Cavanagh won the day for the Houston-based energy giant. The PUC approved the merger, and it wasn't long before the darkest suspicions of Enron's plans were vindicated. The company raised rates, tried to soak the ratepayers with the cost of its failed Trojan nuclear reactor and moved to put some of PGE's most valuable assets on the block. Enron's motive had indeed been to get access to the hydropower of the Northwest, the cheapest in the country, and sell it into the California market, the priciest and-in part because of Cavanagh's campaigning for deregulation-a ripe energy prize awaiting exploitation.

Then, after two years, the company Cavanagh had hailed as being "engaged and motivated" put PGE up on the auction block. Pending sale of PGE, Enron has been using it as collateral for loans approved by a federal bankruptcy judge. In the meantime, Enron continued to bilk the citizens of Oregon. Enron ordered PGE to raise rates in Portland purportedly to cover taxes owed by Enron that were unrelated to PGE business. The rates went up by $35 million. Enron executives pocketed the millions. The taxes were never paid.

Enron is best known as George W. Bush's prime financial backer. But it was a bipartisan purveyor of patronage: to its right, conservative Texas Senator Phil Gramm; to its left, liberal Texas Democrat Sheila Jackson-Lee (who had Enron's CEO Ken Lay as her finance chairman in a Democratic primary fight preluding her first successful Congressional bid; her Democratic opponent was Craig Washington, an anti-NAFTA maverick Democrat the Houston establishment didn't care for).

In the late 1990s, Cavanagh, backed by money from the Energy Foundation, marshaled environmental support for the disastrous scheme to deregulate California's electric utilities, a prize long sought by the state's two biggest power companies, Pacific Gas and Electric and Southern California Edison.

It so happens that the CEO of Southern California Edison is a lawyer named John Bryson, who in the early 1970s started a little environmental outfit with another lawyer named John Adams. That group, of course, was NRDC. According to journalist Sharon Beder, Cavanagh considers himself a protégé of the utility mogul.

In support of the deregulation scheme, Cavanagh argued that regulation of the utilities was passé. In plaintive tones, he promised that after deregulation the competitive forces unleashed by the free market would keep a lid on prices, discourage new nuclear plants, and provide an incentive for conservation and renewable energy sources. Enough people bought this line to allow the deregulation bill to slip through the General Assembly.

None of Cavanagh's promises materialized. Instead, rates and power company profits soared and released from the scrutiny of regulators corporate attention to the reliability of the power grid wilted and California was hit with a series of blackouts in the summers of 2000 and 2001.

Like jackals sniffing a fresh kill, there circling the carnage were Cavanagh's old pals from Enron, who had been freed to prey on the newly deregulated California energy market. Remember Cavanagh's pledge that "You can trust Enron". Now, thanks to a lawsuit brought by Judicial Watch, we have tapes of Enron executives plotting how they could prolong the misery of California residents and maximize their own profits.

One of the big concerns raised by consumer advocates and environmentalists about deregulation was the issue of reliability. Once, freed from obligations imposed by regulators would private companies, driven solely by the profit motive, have an incentive to maintain power lines and power plants to keep them in working order. Yes, said Cavanagh. It turned out quite differently. The companies actually had an incentive to turn the plants off at the precise moment demand was at a peak. In one of the tape-recorded conversations, two Enron executives are heard plotting to raise prices by shutting down a steamer at a power plant.

"I was wondering, um, the demand out there is er ... there's not much, ah, demand for power at all and we're running kind of fat", one executive complains. "Um, if you took down the steamer, how long would it take to get it back up?"

"Oh, it's not something you want to just be turning on and off every hour. Let's put it that way", another Enron employee replies.

"If we shut it down, could you bring it back up in three — three or four hours, something like that?" the executive asks.

"Oh, yeah", the other says.

"Well, why don't you just go ahead and shut her down, then, if that's OK", David says.

On another occasion, two energy traders are joking about how Enron manipulated the prices for electricity in California.

"They're taking all that fucking money back?" says one energy trader to an Enron executive. "All the money you guys stole from those poor grandmothers of California?"

"Yeah, Grandma Millie, man", the Enron executive replies. "But she's the one who couldn't figure out how to fucking vote on the butterfly ballot".

"Now she wants her money back for all the power you've charged right up, jammed right up her ass for $250 a megawatt hour", the other trader chuckled.

The Enron traders loved the blackouts, because that meant they could cash in on the skyrocketing prices helpless consumers were forced to pay. "Just cut 'em off", one Enron executive said. "They're so fucked. They should just bring back fucking horses and carriages, fucking lamps, fucking kerosene lamps".

When wildfires threatened to incinerate power lines and an electric transfer stations, the Enron traders could be heard singing, "Burn, baby, burn".

One Enron employee is heard speaking reverently about one of the most gifted Enron energy traders preying on the California energy crisis.

"He just fucks California", says one Enron employee. "He steals money from California to the tune of about a million".

"Will you rephrase that?" asks a second employee.

"OK, he, um, he arbitrages the California market to the tune of a million bucks or two a day", replies the first. All under the watch of Enron's top executives Jeffrey Skilling and Ken Lay.

Through all of this, John Kerry remained curiously mute. Perhaps because his wife, and chief financial underwriter, Teresa Heinz is not only pals with Cavanagh, but Ken Lay as well.

Teresa Heinz's interest in environmental issues has been mostly expressed through her Heinz Foundation whose board until very recently was adorned by that hero of free-market enviros, Ken Lay of Enron.

The Heinz Foundation put Ken Lay in charge of their global-warming initiative. When Enron went belly up, the Foundation stuck by their man: "Whatever troubles he had at Enron, Ken Lay had a good reputation in the environmental community for being a business man who was environmentally sensitive. When someone does wrong in one part of their life, it doesn't mean they can't do good in another part of their life".

It's the kind of sublime indifference to the messy realities of politics and life that inspired Democrats and environmentalists to rally behind Kerry, under the vacant banner, Anybody But Bush.

● ● ● ● ●

ON MEMORIAL DAY WEEKEND 2004, THE PRICE OF PREMIUM gas in California breached $3 a gallon. Yet, there were no calls for price caps from the Kerry camp and no demand for a criminal investigation into price gouging by the oil cartel. Instead, all Kerry could muster was a limp plea that the strategic petroleum reserves be tapped, an impotent measure unlikely to depress prices by more than two or three cents a gallon for a couple of weeks. But we all know where that oil comes from: drilling on public lands and on the outer continental shelf.

In early June, Kerry raced off to a pow-wow with the American Gas Association, where he reiterated his message to Hoffa that he was ready to drill everywhere, like never before. Shortly afterwards, the trade association issued a smirking press release affirming that Kerry was on board for increased drilling, especially for natural gas.

Back in 1970s, Richard Nixon promoted an energy policy that was far more enlightened than what we now see under Bush or Kerry. And Ken Lay, then a junior staffer at the Federal Energy Commission, had a hand in developing it. Yes, those truly were the good old days.

Chapter 18

"'Write me up some goddamn legislation', Tip O'Neill ordered. 'All anybody in Boston is talking about is Len Bias. They want blood. If we move fast enough we can get out in front of the White House.'"

Alexander Cockburn and Jeffrey St. Clair
Bipartisan Origins of the War on Drugs

ALEXANDER COCKBURN AND JEFFREY ST. CLAIR

Bipartisan Origins
of the War on Drugs

I N 1930 A NEW DEPARTMENT OF THE FEDERAL GOVERNMENT, the Bureau of Narcotics and Dangerous Drugs, was created under the leadership of Harry Anslinger to carry out the war against drug users. Anslinger, an avowed racist, was an adroit publicist and became the prime shaper of American attitudes about drug addiction, hammering home his view that this was not a treatable addiction but a deviant urge that could only be suppressed by harsh criminal sanctions.

Anslinger's first major campaign was to criminalize the drug commonly known at the time as hemp. But Anslinger renamed it "marijuana" to associate it with Mexican laborers who, like the Chinese before them, were unwelcome competitors for scarce jobs in the Depression. Anslinger claimed that marijuana "can arouse in blacks and Hispanics a state of menacing fury or homicidal attack. During this period, addicts have perpetrated some of the most bizarre and fantastic offenses and sex crimes known to police annals."

Anslinger linked marijuana with jazz and persecuted many black musicians, including Thelonious Monk, Dizzy Gillespie and Duke Ellington. Louis Armstrong was also arrested on drug charges, and Anslinger made sure his name was smeared in the press. In Congress, the drug czar testified that "coloreds with big lips lure white women with jazz and marijuana".

By the 1950s, amid the full blast of the Cold War, Anslinger was working with the CIA to charge that the new-born People's Republic of China was attempting to undermine America by selling opium to US crime syndicates. (This took a great deal of chutzpah on the part of the CIA, whose planes were then flying opium from Chiang Kai-Shek's bases in Burma to Thailand and the Philippines for processing and export to the US.) Anslinger convinced the US Senate to approve a resolution stating that "subversion through drug addiction is an established aim of Communist China".

In 1951, Anslinger teamed with Democrat Hale Boggs to marshal through Congress the first minimum mandatory sentences for drug possession: two years for the first conviction for possession of a Schedule 1 drug (marijuana, cocaine), five to ten years for a second offense, and ten to twenty for a third conviction. In 1956 Anslinger once again enlisted the aid of Boggs to pass a law calling for the death penalty to be imposed on anyone selling heroin to a minor, the first linking of drugs with Death Row.

This was Anslinger's last hurrah. Along John Kennedy's New Frontier cantered sociologists attacking Anslinger's punitive philosophy. The tempo of the times changed, and federal money began to target treatment and prevention as much as enforcement and prison. But the interim didn't last long. With the waning of the war in Southeast Asia millions of addicted GIs came home to be ambushed by Richard Nixon's War on Drugs program. Nixon resurrected Anslinger's techniques of threat inflation, declaring in Los Angeles that "as I look over the problems of this country I see that one stands out particularly: the problems of narcotics."

Nixon pledged to launch a war on drugs, to return to the punitive approach and not let any quaint notions of civil liberties and constitutional rights stand in the way. After a Nixon briefing in 1969, his top aide, H.R. Haldeman noted in his diary: "Nixon emphasized that you have to face the fact that the whole problem is really the blacks. The key is to devise a system that recognizes this while not appearing to." And the Democratic congress played along.

But for all of his bluster, Nixon was a mere prelude to the full fury of the Reagan-Bush-Clinton years, when the War on Drugs became explicitly a war on blacks. The first move of the Reagan administration was to expand the drug forfeiture laws, first passed in the Carter administration. In 1981 Reagan's drug policy advisors outlined a plan they thought would be little more than a good PR sound bite, a public display of the required toughness. They proposed allowing the Justice Department to seize real property and so-called "substitute property" – that is, legally acquired assets equal in value to illegal monetary gains. They also proposed that the federal government be permitted to seize attorney's fees that they suspected might have been paid for through drug proceeds. The Reagan plan was to permit forfeitures on the basis of a "probable cause showing" before a federal judge. This meant that seizures could be made against people neither charged nor convicted, but only suspected, of drug offenses.

Contrary to the administration's expectations, this plan sailed through Congress, eagerly supported by two Democratic Party liberals, Senators Hubert Humphrey and Joe Biden, the latter being the artificer in the Carter era of a revision of the RICO statutes, a huge extension of the federal conspiracy laws. Over the next few years the press would occasionally report on some exceptionally bizarre application of the new forfeiture provisions, such as the confiscation of a $25 million yacht in a drug bust that netted only a handful of marijuana stems and seeds. But typically, the press ignored the essential pattern of humdrum seizures, which more often focused on such ordinary assets as houses and cars. For example, in Orange County, California, fifty-seven cars were seized in drug-related cases in 1989 alone. "Even if only a small amount of drugs is found inside," an Orange County narcotics detective explained, "the law permits seized vehicles to be sold by law enforcement agencies to finance anti-drug law enforcement programs."

In fact, the forfeiture program became a tremendous revenue stream for the police. From 1982 to 1991, the US Department of

Justice seized more than $2.5 billion in assets. The feds confiscated $500 million in property in 1991 alone, and 80 percent of these seizures came from people who were never charged with a crime.

On June 17, 1986, University of Maryland basketball star Len Bias died, reportedly from an overdose of cocaine. As Dan Baum put it in his excellent book *Smoke and Mirrors: the War on Drugs and the Politics of Failure*, "In life, Len Bias was a terrific basketball player. In death he became the Archduke Ferdinand of the Total War on Drugs." It was falsely reported that Bias had smoked crack cocaine the night before his death. (He had, in fact, sniffed powder cocaine and, according to the coroner, there was no clear link between this usage and the failure of his heart.)

Bias had just signed to play with the Boston Celtics and amid Boston's rage and grief Speaker of the House Tip O'Neill, a representative from Massachusetts, rushed into action. In early July of that year he convened a special meeting of the Democratic Party leadership on the Hill: "Write me up some goddamn legislation," O'Neill ordered. "All anybody in Boston is talking about is Len Bias. They want blood. If we move fast enough we can get out in front of the White House."

The Reagan White House was moving fast itself. Among other things the Drug Enforcement Agency had been instructed to allow ABC News to accompany it on raids against crack houses. "Crack is the hottest combat-reporting story to come along since the end of the Vietnam War", the head of the New York office of the DEA exulted.

All this fed the congressional frenzy to write tougher laws. House Majority leader Jim Wright, the Texas Democrat, called drug abuse "a menace draining away our economy of some $230 billion this year, slowly rotting away the fabric of our society and seducing and killing our young". Not to be outdone, South Carolina Republican Thomas Arnett proclaimed that "drugs are a threat worse than nuclear warfare or any chemical warfare waged on any battlefield".

So the 1986 Anti-Drug Abuse Act was duly passed. It boasted 29 new minimum mandatory sentences. Up until that time in the entire history of the Republic there had been only 56 minimum mandatory sentences. The new law enacted a death penalty provision for drug "king pins" and prohibited parole for even minor possession offenses. But the chief target of the bill was crack cocaine. Congress established a 100-to-1 sentencing ratio between the possession of crack and powder cocaine. Under this provision, possession of five grams of crack carries a minimum sentence five years in federal prison. The same mandatory minimum is not reached for any amount of powder cocaine under 500 grams. John Kerry voted for the measure.

The sentencing disparity in the 1986 law was based on faulty testimony that crack was fifty times as addictive as powder cocaine. Congress then doubled this ratio as a so-called "violence penalty". Yet there is no inherent difference between the drugs, as Clinton drug czar Barry McCaffrey was forced to admit. The federal Sentencing Commission, established by Congress to review sentencing guidelines, found that so-called "crack violence" was largely attributable to the drug trade itself and has more to do with the setting in which crack is sold than the drug itself: crack is sold on the street, while powder cocaine is often vended by house calls.

As Nixon and Haldeman would have approvingly noted, Tip O'Neill's new drug law was aimed squared at blacks, reminiscent of the early targeting of Chinese smoking opium rather than post-bellum ladies sipping their laudanum-laced tonics.

In 1995 the US Sentencing Commission reviewed eight years of application of this provision and found it to be undeniably racist in practice: 84 percent of those arrested for crack possession where black, while only 10 percent were white and 5 percent Hispanic. The disparity for trafficking arrests was even wider: 88 percent blacks, 7 percent Hispanics and 4 percent whites. By comparison, defendants arrested for powder cocaine possession were 58 percent white, 26 percent black and 15 percent Hispanic.

In Los Angeles all twenty-four federal defendants in crack cases in 1991 were black. The Sentence Commission recommended to Congress that the ratio should be one-to-one between sentences for offenses involving crack and powder cocaine, arguing that federal law allows for other factors to be considered by judges in lengthening sentences (such as whether guns or violence was associated with the offense). But for the first time in its history the Congress rejected the recommendations of the Sentencing Commission and retained the 100-to-1 ratio. Clinton likewise declined the advise of his drug czar and his attorney general and signed the bill.

One need only look at the racial make-up of federal prisons to appreciate the consequences of the 1986 drug law. In 1983 the total number of prisoners in federal, state and local prisons and jails was 600,800. Of those, 57,975 (8.8 percent) were incarcerated for drug-related offenses. In 1993 the total prison population stood at 1.4 million, of whom 353,564—25.1 percent—were inside for drug offenses. The Sentencing Project, a DC-based watchdog group, found that the increase was far from racially balanced. Between 1986 and 1991 the incarceration rate for white males convicted on drug crimes increased by 106 percent. But the number of black males in prison for kindred offenses soared by a factor of 429 percent, and the rate for black women went up by an incredible 828 percent.

The queen of the drug war, Nancy Reagan, said amid one of her innumerable sermons on the issue: "If you're a casual drug user, you're an accomplice to murder." In tune with this line of thinking, the Democratic-controlled Congress moved in 1988 to expand the crimes for which the federal death penalty could be imposed. These included drug-related murders, and murders committed by drug gangs, which would allow any gang member to face the death penalty if one member of the gang was linked to a drug killing. The new penalties were inscribed in an update of the Continuing Criminal Enterprises Act.

Convictions under the new law between 1989 and 1996 were 70 percent white and 24 percent black. But 90 percent of the times the federal prosecutors sought the death penalty it was against non-whites: of these, 78 percent were black and the rest Hispanic. From 1930 to 1972 (when the Supreme Court found the death penalty unconstitutional), 85 percent of those given death sentences were white. When the federal death penalty was reapplied in 1984, with the Anti-Drug Abuse Act, the numbers for black death penalty convictions soared. Of those on Death Row, both federal and state, 50 percent are black, although blacks constitute only 16 percent of the US population.

Chapter 19

"Integration, therefore, at this turn of the century, has become another promise, not exactly broken, but finagled to mean whatever does not cross the borders of white comfort. Perhaps separate can be equalized after all."

Greg Moses
Civil Rights Down Through the Presidencies

Civil Rights Down Through the Presidencies

WHITE AMERICA BREATHED A SIGH OF DENIAL IN 1980 when Ronald Reagan proclaimed during his campaign for president that he could not recall any racial tensions at his boyhood town of Dixon, Illinois. Whew. Thank God. During all those turbulent years of civil rights struggle, we as a people had been worried about nothing at all.

Reagan's civil rights record is summed up by the Law Enforcement Legal Defense Fund, which brags that today's board member, William Bradford Reynolds, when serving as Reagan's Assistant Attorney General for Civil Rights, "fought against reverse discrimination, quotas and similar policies".

Indeed, author Raymond Wolters reports that Reynolds was Reagan's chief of civil rights for eight years: "His tenure lasted longer than that of any other occupant of the office since its creation under the Civil Rights Act of 1957. A descendant both of the Puritan religious leader, Governor William Bradford of Massachusetts, and of the Du Pont family of industrialists, Reynolds reflected the ideological bent and political wishes of the president who appointed him. This meant an association with a chief executive who believed that the civil rights revolution had not only gone too far but had subverted the constitutional guarantees designed to ensure racial equality."

As the first Bush White House entered mid-term, an enterprising group of anti-civil rights lawyers set up shop as the Center for Individual Rights. We'll let the Center's website do all the bragging: "Its small revenue base notwithstanding, 1989 was a good year to have opened a conservative public interest firm. The Reagan Administration had just ended and the number of conservative lawyers in the for-profit sector had increased. Many partners and associates shared the Center's ideals and objectives and were eager to help with its cases."

By the end of the Reagan decade, reasearchers Douglass Massey and Nancy Denton found hypersegregation in the Frost Belt cities of Baltimore, Chicago, Cleveland, Detroit, Milwaukee and Philadelphia. And that was before a further decade of resegregation in employment and education.

To be sure, African American neighborhoods have been self-selected and self-organized for centuries, but federal policies still discourage equal opportunity in housing by "subsidizing suburban growth at the expense of urban areas, supporting racial covenants by denying African Americans mortgage insurance in integrated communities, providing mortgage insurance in segregated residential areas, and redlining", the US Commission on Civil Rights reported in October, 2003.

As it turns out, passion for integration in education lasted among white folks only long enough to replace black teachers. Once the jobs were secured, white teachers joined their race cohorts in flight to the suburbs where they could commute to work until something closer came up. So here's your updated glossary. Integration means replacing black teachers. When it comes to including black teachers or black students, that's called reverse discrimination.

Integration, therefore, at this turn of the century, has become another promise, not exactly broken, but finagled to mean whatever does not cross the borders of white comfort. Perhaps separate can be equalized after all.

In higher education, regents at the University of California led a retreat in 1995, when they abandoned affirmative action, even prior to a state referendum, Prop. 209, that asserted the state's right to opt out of affirmative action altogether.

And the Texas higher education de-segregation plan of 2000, orchestrated by Governor Bush, codified perfectly the post-*Brown* retreat. With the pressure taken off of historically white colleges to integrate, thanks to the *Hopwood* ruling by three West Texas judges in 1996, the Texas de-segregation plan instead turned to long-neglected budgets of the state's two black universities, Texas Southern and Prairie View.

Later, when the Supreme Court barely vindicated affirmative action in 2003, many Texas universities returned to the practice, with the notable exception of Texas A&M University, led by Clear Channel CEO Lowry Mays, acting as chairman of the regents, and former CIA director Robert Gates, acting as university president – Bush clansmen both.

In 1990, President Bush had chimed in with the theme of Presidential regression when he vetoed one bill for civil rights but signed another in favor of mandatory sentencing, fostering practical directions for political leadership that the Clinton administration did not contravene.

In 1993, Clinton raised hopes for dramatic changes in Washington leadership, when he nominated Lani Guinier as "the first black woman to head the Civil Rights Division of the Department of Justice". But the idea was so intolerable to official Washington that Clinton abandoned the nomination before the hearings got started.

Although Clinton's second choice, Bill Lann Lee, was sharp and active, and although Guinier eventually landed on her tenured feet at Harvard Law School, vital intellectual challenges to the structure of racialized injustice remained pretty narrowly focused or confined to academic journals. And for the rest of the Clinton presidency, vacancies marked the spot of hesitation in crucial civil rights appointments.

In 1994, two months prior to the Republican resurgence in Congress, Clinton put his signature on a bill that eliminated federal tuition for prison education. As reported by John Garmon in *Black Issues for Higher Education*, "In 1990, there were 350 higher education programs for inmates. In 1997, there were only eight".

Yet according to the Contract with America that was being widely distributed in advance of the 1994 November campaign for Republican restoration, Clinton had taken the "liberal" road. Point two in the contract called for, "The Taking Back our Streets Act: An anti-crime package including stronger truth-in-sentencing, 'good faith' exclusionary rule exemptions, effective death penalty provisions, and cuts in social spending from this summer's 'crime' bill to fund prison construction and additional law enforcement to keep people secure in their neighborhoods and kids safe in their schools".

The Contract with America included no mention of civil rights. "Mend it, don't end it" was the best Clinton could come up with as he defended affirmative action in 1995, pointing out that from every $1,000 spent by the Department of Education, forty cents went to programs "targeted at underrepresented minorities". Forty cents. Surely this is Klan accounting at its best, precisely mocking the long-broken promise of forty acres and a mule. Forty cents on the thousand.

According to a timeline posted at greatbooks.com, 1995 is the year that, for many states, "there emerges for the first time a nearly dollar-for-dollar tradeoff between corrections and education spending. New York, for example, steadily increased its Department of Corrections budget by 76 percent to $761 million. During the same period, the state decreased funding to its city and state university systems by 28 percent, to $615 million". And 1994 in California "was the first time the state's corrections budget exceeded that of the entire University of California system", reports jail educator Christina Boufis.

By 1998, "six years into the President's term", argued the Citizens' Commission for Civil Rights, "while the President continues to speak with understanding and empathy about the plight of people trapped in racial and economic isolation, he and his Administration have yet to provide clear direction with respect to civil rights policy".

White people were still turbulent on the question of race, with a majority of white voters in Louisiana favoring a well-known Klan activist for Governor in 1990. The founder of the National Association for the Advancement of White People was defeated by the remaining plurality of white voters, combined with black and Hispanic constituencies. Yet his official website is up and running still.

National debates about race were stirred by camcorder images of Rodney King's beating in March 1991, then by news helicopters broadcasting riots as soon as the police defendants were declared not guilty in April 1992. The "white flight" jury of Simi Valley had, in the words of Akira Mizuta Lippit, decided not to apply the law, but to "evaluate the status of the law itself". White flight is still based on a social subjectivity that demands a license to brutalize.

The O.J. Simpson jury was sequestered on January 11, 1995. On October 2 they took four hours to find him not guilty. In 1997, a civil jury found Simpson liable for $8.5 million in damages. His estate was sold off and demolished. But the experience of the televised criminal trial, and the polarized responses it evoked from black and white audiences, linger with memories of Rodney King as sensational exhibits of a visceral divide between black and white communities in the matter of police relations.

In August 1997, the Haitian immigrant Abner Louima was raped with a broom handle by at least one New York City policeman. Of the four officers initially implicated in the case, one pled guilty and was sentenced to thirty years. Another made a deal for five years' time. The other two saw their convictions for obstruction set aside, and they were last seen in March 2004, suing for "full retroactive pay, benefits and seniority".

Then on June 6, 1998, James Byrd was killed and dragged behind a pickup truck in Jasper, Texas, an hour's drive north of the Klan's famous holdout at Vidor. When the Klan rallied in support of the three defendants, who were said to be connected to white racist groups in prison, about 200 anti-Klan protesters met them at the Jasper town square.

All three of Byrd's killers were convicted, two of them sentenced to Texas' infamous death row. And wariness in relation to white power was summed up by 72-year-old Unav Wade, who told the Associated Press that based on his experience in Alabama, California, and Texas, the only mistake the killers made was to drag their evidence through the black parts of town. Had the crime been done in a white neighborhood, "they'd have covered it up and we'd have never known".

This chilling litany of sensational images is both instructive and misleading. Overt, acknowledged barbarity can be racism's best friend, if we forget the commonplaces that are both better and worse.

It is not facile to point out that while all these violent outbreaks were swirling in the American mind, Oprah Winfrey built a colossal national reputation and fortune by presenting herself on television every day of the year, Cornel West rose to prominence as national philosopher, and John Hope Franklin convened an important federal conversation on race.

And it is crucial to assess the future potential of black politics in terms of the influence and power that is being earned by Hip Hop artists and managers, exemplified by the life and work of Russell Simmons.

But it does appear that the White House has been rather listless, and Congress unreliable, because the American people themselves, especially white Americans, have not yet made themselves into a nation that digs where the digging is needed, despite the resources that have long been available for the work.

Opinion polls continue to show that whites always report more optimism than blacks when it comes to assessing how far we've come. David Bositis, the essential researcher for the essential think tank, the Joint Center for Political and Economic

Studies says: "Most white people do not have firsthand experiences with racism. Most or all black people, in fact, do. Because black people do have that experience with racism, they are intensely conscious of the significance of racism and its impact on American society". In contrast, many white Americans "don't recognize that it's a problem. They don't recognize its reality…. And if it's not a problem, nothing needs to be done to remedy it."

And racism does not stand alone or isolated. Police, prisons, employment, housing, poverty, health, and environmental hazards are some of the larger institutions that remain stubbornly unaffected, because of the era of denial that Reagan launched and that Clinton couldn't, or wouldn't overcome.

The policies of the second Bush administration trace the trajectory of Reagan and Bush before him. Since the Texas A&M campus, for instance, is one location that is culturally and politically suited to Bush influence, we learn a lot from the fact that Lowry Mays and Robert Gates upheld the *Hopwood* inertia. One quiet phone call from the White House is all it would take to turn things another way.

John Kerry was given attention for his hand-wringing speeches during the 1990s that were much consistent with Clinton's "mend it, don't end it" theme. But as one Republican gadfly to the US Commission on Civil Rights complained in an article for *National Review*: "While Kerry claims he seeks to 'mend, not end' affirmative action and that he rejects quotas, he's done neither. In the 12 years since the Yale speech, Kerry's had numerous opportunities to vote against quotas and 'mend' affirmative action, yet in every case he's stuck with the status quo, i.e., in favor of quotas and set asides". By the lights of Peter Kirsanow, Kerry counts for a hypocrite. And maybe that's true.

Voters seemed to agree that Bush speaks more plainly than Kerry. So the choice in November between Kerry and Bush was between a hypocrite who voted for civil rights and a plain talker who organized against it. If there was moral leadership here, it is something besides second best.

Returning to that group of conservative attorneys once groomed by the Reagan-Bush team, we find that Clarence Thomas was appointed to the Supreme Court in 1991. Ted Olson, who argued for *Hopwood* and helped win the acquittals for the Rodney King beating, now serves as Solicitor General, where he argues on behalf of the USA, before Thomas and associates, that affirmative action is reverse discrimination.

And the Center for Individual Rights has filed a class action suit that, "challenges employment goals and preferences for women and minorities at two federal agencies, Housing and Urban Development, and the Equal Employment Opportunity Commission.

Having lost ground since *Hopwood* and *Grutter v. Bollinger*, the center is also back in the face of higher education, arguing that pre-1998 admissions standards at the University of Washington School of Law were unconstitutional. And they may be correct about that. Even the *Hopwood* ruling was correct in finding that the quotas then being used by the University of Texas Law School were peculiarly un-constitutional. But the Center does not seek these opportunities for the purpose of "mending" affirmative action. They want to end it. And the moral bankruptcy of their contribution to history will lie alongside well-known graves.

Since the 13th, 14th, and 15th Amendments were adopted after the Civil War, only the parties have changed sides, not the moral worth of the social relations intended, or the persistent reaction against them.

Election year politics for civil rights therefore revolve around the crucial institutions of the executive branch and Congress. Who gets elected will help determine the quality of laws and appointments. Who gets encouraged will have effects on the kind of talent that a decade from now will set up legal foundations in Washington. These in turn will continue to have some effect on the direction of the Courts. But gurgling beneath all these foundations of modern power is the winding river, the people asking themselves, who do We The People want America to be?

Chapter 20

"In the Bush-Clinton-Bush years, the number of incarcerated people per 100,000 US resident increased from 163 to 231. We hold the record in this category. The parties do not differ on the issue of prisons, because both are wedded to corporate power, and the prisons, for that power, provide a vital service."

Vijay Prashad
Capitalism's Warehouses

VIJAY PRASHAD
Capitalism's Warehouses

BILL CLINTON ALWAYS CULTIVATED THE IMAGE OF BEING the boy from Hope who made good, who understood that the state could be an oasis in the factory desert of late industrial capitalism. On a chilly January morning in 1993, he called on Americans to "celebrate the mystery of American renewal".

> This new world [after the fall of the USSR] has already enriched the lives of millions of Americans who are able to compete and win in it. But when most people are working harder for less; when others cannot work at all; when the cost of health care devastates families and threatens to bankrupt many of our enterprises, great and small; when fear of crime robs law abiding citizens of their freedom; and when millions of poor children cannot even imagine the lives we are calling them to lead – we have not made change our friend. We know we have to face hard truths and take strong steps. But we have not done so. Instead we have drifted, and that drifting has eroded our resources, fractured our economy, and shaken our confidence.... Let us resolve to make our government a place for what Franklin Roosevelt called 'bold, persistent experimentation,' a government for our tomorrows, not our yesterdays.

Some Americans have done well, yes, but many struggle and suffer. They have little hope, and little confidence in the capacity of the state to deliver social justice. A powerful civil rights movement had thriven with the assumption that if people won their rights in the state, the state would be able to ensure that those rights would be translated into a share of the social wealth and social dignity. The struggle produced the rights, but the state's priorities changed in the process. It did not fail people because some bad individuals had taken power of the state, or because people did not have the imagination to act in any other way. What had happened as soon as the people won their rights is that corporate power did its utmost to void the state of any content, indeed, it disemboweled the state. They privatized the public commons (such as education and electricity) and impoverished the concept of the "citizen". If the state is no longer capable of being the regulator of power and the disseminator of social goods, then what does citizenship mean? To demand rights from such state is akin to banging on a door to an empty room.

Those who listened to Clinton's speech from behind bars would have already picked up the code and shuddered: he used the word "crime", and he put petty criminality on par with the lack of health care and the lack of living wages (which are the masterful crimes of capitalism). If he could do nothing against corporate power, he took out his wrath on petty criminals. When Clinton came to office, the correctional system supervised 4.5 million Americans, but when he left the number increased to 6.4 million. Clinton is the Prisons President.

Eight years later, in January 2001, the un-elected George W. Bush stood at the same spot. Aware of the explosion of prisons nationwide, and in his own state of Texas, Bush offered these words: "In the quiet of American conscience, we know that deep, persistent poverty is unworthy of our nation's promise...And the proliferation of prisons, however necessary, is no substitute for hope and order in our souls". The meaningful phrase here was "however necessary". As Governor of Texas, Bush signed the final orders for the execution of one hundred and fifty-two prisoners in five years. His prisons held women in "detention trailers", where, under the hot sun of Texas, the guards did not allow them water. According to the Texas Prison Labor Union and various human rights groups, the prison guards in a number of Texas prisons sexually assaulted prisoners, beat them, forced them to crawl in the dirt, set dogs on them and shot them with stun guns. In 1999, a US judge found that

Texas prisons cultivate a "culture of sadistic and malicious violence". In his tenure as President, the jail population increased further, and whereas during the Clinton years the annual average increase of incarcerated people was 4.3%, in the Bush years, it rose to 5.4 percent.[1] Bush is a more enthusiastic Clinton.

In the Bush-Clinton-Bush years, the number of incarcerated people per 100,000 US resident increased from 163 to 231. We hold the record in this category. The parties do not differ on the issue of prisons, because both are wedded to corporate power, and the prisons, for that power, provide a vital service.

As the US economy's productive sector reorganized in the 1970s and 1980s, the working class was forced to relocate, downward. Workers in manufacturing had previously earned a decent union wage with benefits, and white workers gained immeasurably from their access to federal credit to buy homes and other assets in the 1950s and early 1960s (before the Equal Rights Act).[2] With the formal victories of the Civil Rights Act, black workers and other non-white workers, fought to get jobs in the protected sector just as globalization devastated the very sectors that promised them freedom. First, the big plants began to close down in the shake-down of Reagan-era structural adjustment. Second, non-white workers thronged into union jobs at the many municipalities and state administrations (and then, into AFSCME), but at this very time, the government began to shrink social services and cut back on these jobs.

As industrial devastation proceeded apace, those without employment either turned to "contingent" work or else to the government for social welfare. The latter grew in name in the 1960s with the Great Society Programs, but it was always a small check for each household, precious funds, but never anything to be too excited about, so that even those eligible for welfare worked off the books to supplement their household income. Everyone from the class that began to go to jail and to prison had some form of contingent job or another. Contract labor, piece-work (including housework, childcare as well as manufacturing outwork) and temporary labor are not new forms of labor, but they are increasingly becoming the paradigm for the US workforce. F. W. Taylor and Henry Ford would not recognize today's economy that relies less on factory discipline than on the discipline of hunger. Contractors or jobbers offer a hard-pressed population work under unenviable conditions and the employers rely upon the desperation of their "outworkers" to produce the quotas. Healthcare, vacation time, etc. are the responsibility of the worker; the employer takes the best products, rejects the bad ones, and does not hire the worker during lean times or if the worker is ill.

In 1994, the Bureau of Labor Statistics reported that temporary agencies accounted for fifteen percent of the new jobs created in 1993, and twenty-six percent of the new jobs created in 1992. In 1989, temporary agencies accounted for less than three percent of the new jobs. A generation of temporary workers was now moving into the workforce. Soon, twenty-five percent of the workforce was employed in such conditions and they cost forty percent less than full-time permanent employees.

Data from 1995 show us that the typical contingent worker was black, female, young, enrolled in school and employed in the service sector or in construction.[3] About ten percent of the contingent workers were teachers. In February 1995, the contingent workforce totaled between 2.7 and 6 million workers (depending upon whether the totals included those who were in a job for a year by choice or not by choice), but the government added another 6.5 million because of workers who toil at multiple jobs and are therefore not counted in the Current Population Survey as "contingent workers." Of the latter, the multiple-job holders, the most common characteristic was that they are young, mainly women.[4] While the literature is divided on the reasons for such an extensive turn to part-time work, the most compelling argument is that "the use of contingent work has arisen because of the decline in unionism, which permits firms to take advantage of the cost savings embodied in more flexible staffing arrangements".[5] While this is so, it fails to engage with the broad shifts in the economy, with the deterioration of manufacturing within the US and with a general tendency toward making the productive process efficient for capital generation and not for social welfare.

The class of the "contingent" generally enters the vice economy not for malevolent reasons, but typically to supplement a major decline in household income. Many studies show that urban blacks nourish a desire not just to hold a job, but for worthwhile work and education, for a meaningful life. Significant numbers of those who are in poverty, further, are transients between meaningless jobs. There is widespread recognition in the literature of the distress and disaffection among urban (that is, working-class) blacks and of their desires and struggles to fashion a destiny.[6] Even Bill Clinton's advisor on race, now Harvard professor William Wilson argued in a popular book from 1996, "A neighborhood in which people are poor but employed is different from a neighborhood in which people are poor and jobless. Many of today's problems in the inner-city ghetto neighborhoods – crime, family dissolution, welfare, low levels of social organization, and so on – are fundamentally a consequence of the disappearance of work."[7] His advisee, President Clinton, did not pay much heed to this argument.

If the class of the contingent must be left outside the ken of work, there is a high chance that they will demand collective power or your individual wallet or pocket book or the cash tills of 7/11s and fast food outlets whose check out clerks stand as much as five times as much chance of being killed on the job as any cop in the line of duty. Both political rebellion and individual criminality become a problem of the social order created by the dominant classes. As the political scientist and co-founder of the Black Radical Congress, Manning Marable put it, "Prisons have become the method for keeping hundreds of thousands of potentially rebellious, dissatisfied, and alienated black youth off the streets."[8] The US state will continue the process of controlling disgruntled and politically angry populations by the threat of prison and by the politics of "realism" that moves dissatisfied Americans to discourage an analysis of their situation and to lay the blame for their ills on immigrants, on the poor and on the non-white.

To recover profits US managers and financiers pushed the manufacturing sector toward greater mechanization as well as toward extracting more toil from fewer workers, the latter being code-named "productivity gain". On the latter point, workers in fast food restaurants, for instance, have to get ready for work before they can clock in (rather than clocking in and then using work time to put on their uniforms), they cannot do any personal things on the clock, and in many firms, workers have to clock out to take a bathroom break.[9] The more efficient use of the workforce allowed firms to release a large number of surplus workers into the world of the unemployed, the underemployed, the contingent, and the two-job crew. How is this vast section of humanity to survive in cities and small towns whose bureaucracies have made it impossible to build shantytowns, beg on the streets and be fed by the charity of restaurants? Who will pay for the upkeep of this reserve army, this unemployed and shiftless population? Families can no longer absorb the costs, as more and more members of the household take up less and less lucrative jobs. With the stock market in turbulence from the late 1990s, the real estate markets absorbed much of the capital and produced a boom in property. While the link between the real estate market and rental property is not direct, there has been a secular rise in rents across the country.[10] With high rents, landlords are very strict about how many people camp out in an apartment. Small motels and courageous families become the homes of those who once held steady jobs. Stagnating wages and escalating real estate prices have raised the problem to "crisis proportions." A local journalist in Telluride, Colorado pointed out that homelessness "brings instability and a surly work force. We can't expect nice worker attitudes when people come to work begging a shower". In the same town, a worker in a shop who sleeps in a sleeping bag during -40 Degree Fahrenheit nights had a very different perspective: "The town doesn't realize that the people who do their dishes and clean up after them have to live someplace too."[11] Welfare, or state financial support, slowly dried up. Obsessed with overturning Reagan's deficit spending of the 1980s, the Clinton-era managers of the U.S. economy were bent on cutting Government spending. Rather than touch the military (one component of stabilization), subsidies to farmers or subsidies in the form of tax breaks to corporations, they ended the social safety net for the working poor and the disabled in 1996.[12] Who, then, is to feed, clothe and shelter the reserve army of labor?

As more people go to jail each year, it becomes the storehouse of the redundant working population as well as its soup kitchen. The state prefers to provide social services to the unemployed if they submit themselves to total surveillance: prison is the ultimate place for such debasement. As the contingent class grew in the early 1990s, the government slashed its social security net (welfare) and opted to deal with the indigent via prisons. The state did not stop spending funds, but it simply redirected its social welfare money toward incarceration. Instead of juicing up the economy by cash disbursements to the working-class (demand side growth generation), the government preferred to offer the taxes it collects toward its own state enterprises (prisons, etc.) or else to private businesses who either run prisons or else work in the construction and maintenance of them (supply side growth generation). Here is Angela Davis, former political prisoner, professor at the University of

California-Santa Cruz, and founder of Critical Resistance (a group committed to the abolition of prisons):

> Imprisonment has become the response of first resort to far too many of the social problems that burden people who are ensconced in poverty. These problems often are veiled by being conveniently grouped together under the category 'crime' and by the automatic attribution of criminal behavior to people of color. Homelessness, unemployment, drug addiction, mental illness, and illiteracy are only a few of the problems that disappear from public view when the human beings contending with them are relegated to cages....
> Colored bodies constitute the main human raw material in this vast experiment to disappear the major social problems of our time. Once the aura of magic is stripped away from the imprisonment solution, what is revealed is racism, class bias and the parasitic seduction of capitalist profit.[13]

In 1993, the state spent more on Aid to Families with Dependent Children (AFDC) than on corrections, but by 1996 (on the other side of the Crime Bill) the priority was reversed. The government added more than $8 billion to corrections in this period, while it slashed AFDC by almost $2 billion. Gregory Winter, who works at the Hamilton Family Center in San Francisco, spells out the arithmetic, "When funds are siphoned away from social programs to prisons, communities are drawn inexorably toward incarceration." Furthermore if incarceration trumps social security at the same pace, "the criminal justice system will become the government's primary interface with poor communities, particularly those of color. Prisons will replace public entitlements, subsidized housing, and perhaps even the schools as the principle place where poor people converge."[14]

In 1993, Clinton was right: we need to fashion a government for our tomorrow, not for our yesterdays. This cannot be accomplished in the short-run, because we don't have a strong enough progressive social movement to give substance to such dreams.

Whatever choice we make as Americans in any presidential election has consequences, but there should be no illusions about who will stand in Washington and intone his vision for "our" America. Our America can only emerge from our sustained struggle to reconfigure the relationship between corporate power, the people and the state. As it stands, corporate power wants to warehouse the people who cannot "compete and win" in prisons, and the state does this work for them enthusiastically. We want to abolish the prison. To do so is to abolish the dispensation that we live under in general, the world of the CEO class on the one side and the "contingent" on the other.

[1] All data are from the Bureau of Justice Statistics.

[2] The best summary of this material is in George Lipsitz, *The Possessive Investment in Whiteness*, Philadelphia: Temple University Press, 1998, Chapter 1.

[3] Anna E. Polivka, "A Profile of Contingent Workers," Monthly Labor Review, October 1996.

[4] "A Different Look at Part-Time Employment," *Issues in Labor Statistics*, Department of Labor, Bureau of Labor Statistics, April 1996 and Jackie Chu, Sonya Smallets and Jill Braunstein, The Economic Impact of Continent Work on Women and Their Families,

Washington, DC: Institute for Women's Policy Research, 1995.

[5] Polivka, "A Profile," p. 19 summarizes Lonnie Goldstein and Eileen Applebaum, "What Was Driving the 1982-1988 Boom in Temporary Employment," *American Journal of Economics and Sociology*, October 1992, p. 473.

[6] Much of this work is the result of the New Chicago School, mainly from students of William J. Wilson such as Sudhir Venkatesh (see his two papers, "Getting Ahead: Social Mobility among the urban poor," *Sociological Perspectives*, vol. 37, no. 2, 1994, and "The Social Organization of Street Gang Activity in

the Urban Ghetto," American Journal of Sociology, vol. 103, no. 1, July 1997) and Loic Wacquant, "America as Realized Social Dystopia: the politics of urban disintegration," International Journal of Contemporary Sociology, vol. 34, no. 1, 1997. The philosopher Charles Mills points out that the term used to designate the class of the contingent, the "underclass," operates in popular discourse in such a way as "a class which is not a class, a social entity which is asocial." Charles W. Mills, "Under Class Under Standings," Ethics, vol. 104, July 1994, p. 858.

[7] William Julius Wilson, When Work Disappears. The World of the New Urban Poor, New York: Random House, 1996, p. xiii.

[8] Manning Marable, The Crisis of Color and Democracy, Monroe: Common Courage, 1992, pp. 18-19.

[9] Barbara Ehrenreich's book, Nickle and Dimed, is the best current ethnography of the war over time and space in the service workplace.

[10] David Talbot, "Sky-high Hub rents change face of city," Boston Herald, 3 January 1999; David Benda, "City's Supply of Affordable Housing is Drying Up," Redding Record Searchlight, 11 December 2000; Hisham Aidi, "A 'Second Renaissance' in Harlem?" Africana.Com, 18 December 2000; Brian J. Rogal, "Real Estate Boom Threatens Affordable Housing Options," The Chicago Reporter, November/December 2000.

[11] Gregory Jaynes, "Down and Out in Telluride," Time, 5 September 1994, pp. 60-61.

[12] In the current process of stabilization, there are predominantly three components: Structural Adjustment Programs in the Third World and in Eastern Europe, technological developments of "smart weapons," and down-sizing in businesses in the overdeveloped world. For the purposes of this short book, I am not going to conduct an analysis of the first two components of US stabilization since there is much good work on that found elsewhere. I have covered some of this ground in Fat Cats and Running Dogs, Monroe: Common Courage, 2002.

[13] Angela Y. Davis, "Masked Racism: Reflections on the Prison Industrial Complex," ColorLines, vol. 1, no. 2, Fall 1998, p. 12 and p. 13. For an extension of her crucial arguments about prisons and capitalism, see "From the Prison of Slavery to the Slavery of Prisons: Frederick Douglass and the Convict Lease System" and "Racialized Punishment and Prison Abolition," The Angela Y. Davis Reader, Ed. Joy James, Oxford: Basil Blackwell, 1998.

[14] Gregory Winter, "Trading Places. When Prisons Substitute for Social Programs," ColorLines, vol. 1, no. 2, Fall 1998, p. 22.

Chapter 21

"Presidents come and go, but many policies stay the same. Rand Beers, Kerry's top national security advisor and likely National Security Advisor in a Kerry administration, is a revolving door man. Under Presidents Clinton and Bush, he served as Assistant Secretary of State for International Narcotics and Law Enforcement Affairs, and was one of the chief architects of and apologists for the United States' cruel policies in Colombia."

Sean Donahue
Rand Beers and Colombia

SEAN DONAHUE

Rand Beers and Colombia

WHEN RAND BEERS QUIT HIS JOB AS COUNTER-TERROR-ism advisor to President Bush, and signed up with John Kerry's presidential campaign, he quickly became a hero to Democratic Party loyalists and the "Anybody but Bush" crowd. Presidents come and go, but many policies stay the same. Beers, who has become Kerry's top national security advisor and would likely serve as National Security Advisor or Secretary of State in a Kerry administration, is a revolving door man. Under Presidents Clinton and Bush, he served as Assistant Secretary of State for International Narcotics and Law Enforcement Affairs, and was one of the chief architects of and apologists for the United States' cruel policies in Colombia.

Beers was most closely associated with the disastrous aerial crop fumigation program the U.S. introduced in southern Colombia. The State Department hired DynCorp, a private military contractor, to fly crop dusters at high altitudes over the rainforests of southern Colombia, spraying a chemical cocktail that includes a stronger version of Monsanto's herbicide, Round-Up, over suspected coca fields. Beers was the public face of the fumigation program, defending it in Congressional hearings and in the media.

Touted as a way of stopping cocaine from entering the U.S., the fumigation program targets the poorest people with the least involvement in international drug trafficking – the coca growers – while leaving the cocaine processors and exporters, who make the real profits in the drug trade, untouched. In a good year, a farmer planting 5 acres of coca can bring in $4,000. Once that coca is processed into cocaine and brought to the U.S. it has a street value of close to $800,000. During a visit to Putumayo, the main coca growing area in southern Colombia in 2001, a parish priest told me "We look on in great pain when we see how the farmers are trampled on like cockroaches while the big traffickers walk the streets of New York and L.A."

The processing and export of cocaine are largely controlled by wealthy landowners and the right-wing paramilitaries that support them, while coca growers are "taxed" by the Marxist rebels of the Revolutionary Armed Forces of Colombia (FARC). The paramilitaries are technically considered terrorists by the U.S., but play a significant role in protecting U.S. economic interests by using massacres to clear off land for oil development, logging, hydro-electric dams, and cattle ranching, and by assassinating union organizers, indigenous leaders, and other critics of the political and economic order in Colombia, while the FARC keeps attacking oil pipelines and kidnapping wealthy people – and so the FARC is defined as a "narco-terrorist group", and U.S. policy is focused on weakening the FARC. Fumigating coca crops indirectly cuts into FARC revenues, and so the program is sold to the public as part of both the war on drugs and the war on terrorism. Beers played a central role in creating the myth of the "narco-terrorist" which has been used to justify both the fumigations and continued U.S. military aid to Colombia.

The program has had no measurable impact on the availability, price, or purity of cocaine in the U.S., let alone the rate of cocaine addiction in this country. Historically, whenever coca has been eradicated in one area of the Andes, production has spiked in other areas. The difficult materials for cocaine producers to procure are the chemicals used to process coca into cocaine. But the U.S. has made only minimal efforts to regulate the export of these chemicals.

The farmers who grow coca in southern Colombia are growing it not by choice, but out of necessity. Over 6 percent of Colombians live on less than $2 a day. As a result of economic globalization, the bottom has dropped out of markets for coffee, bananas, wheat, and other legal crops. The soil in Putumayo is poor, anyway, and won't support repeated plantings of most cash crops. And farmers growing legal crops have to transport them over dangerous, poorly maintained dirt roads, while coca buyers are willing to go into remote villages to buy coca leaves and coca paste. None of this means much to Rand Beers, who told ABC's John Stossel that:

"An illegal activity is an illegal activity. And one doesn't get a special pass for being poor. They have to recognize that every effort to grow coca will be challenged by the government. Every work effort, every dollar, every pound of sweat that goes into growing that coca may be lost."

Besides being cruel, Beers' attitude ignores the fact that farmers who don't grow coca have been hurt just as badly by the fumigations as farmers who do grow coca. Glyphosate, the active ingredient in the chemical cocktail used in the fumigation program, is a broad-spectrum herbicide that kills any and all green plants. The crop fumigation planes fly at high altitudes, and so their spraying is at best imprecise. As a result, many farmers growing only legal crops have lost everything.

In January of 2001, I visited a government-funded yucca cooperative that was intended to help farmers find an alternative to growing coca. The cooperative had been fumigated and the entire yucca crop had been destroyed. I met one woman who had invested everything she had in the co-op and now had no way to feed her children. She wanted to go to the city to beg, but couldn't leave town because the paramilitaries who had killed her brothers had a roadblock on the only road out of La Hormiga. Corn and plantain crops on surrounding farms had been destroyed as well. Many people were complaining of rashes, respiratory problems, and temporary blindness caused by the fumigations.

When confronted with these problems, Beers' Colombian counterpart, Gonzalo de Francisco, National Security Advisor to

Colombia's President, replied that "Fumigation is like chemotherapy, sometimes you end up killing the patient." Beers, for his part, consistently denied that there was any evidence that the fumigations were causing health problems. The U.S. State Department and the Colombian government both claim that farmers whose legal crops are fumigated are compensated for their losses, but community organizers in Putumayo report that few if any farmers have actually been compensated, and the U.S. Embassy has been unable to provide any concrete evidence that the compensation program is working.

Beers went even further in defending the fumigation program when he gave a sworn deposition in a lawsuit filed against DynCorp in a U.S. Federal District Court by indigenous tribes in Ecuador. The Indians claimed that their health and their crops had been damaged when herbicides sprayed in Colombia drifted over the border on the wind. Desperate to keep the suit from proceeding to trial, he argued that the fumigation program was vital to U.S. national security because it was an essential part of the war against terrorism in Colombia. He then went a step further, stating, under oath, that "It is believed that FARC terrorists have received training in Al Qaeda terrorist camps in Afghanistan."

Beers' claim was absurd. The idea that Islamic fundamentalists would align themselves with hard line Marxists halfway around the world doesn't even meet the laugh test. An *Associated Press* story on Beers' testimony quoted three baffled Washington insiders:

> 'There doesn't seem to be any evidence of FARC going to Afghanistan to train', a U.S. intelligence official said. 'We have never briefed anyone on that and frankly, I doubt anyone has ever alleged that in a briefing to the State Department or anyone else.'[...] 'That statement is totally from left field', said a top federal law enforcement official, who reviewed the proffer. 'I don't know where (Beers) is getting that. We have never had any indication that FARC

guys have ever gone to Afghanistan.' 'My first reaction was
that Rand must have misspoke', said a veteran congressional
staffer with extensive experience in the Colombian drug war.
'But when I saw it was a proffer signed under oath, I couldn't
believe he would do that. I have no idea why he would say
that.'

Beers later recanted his testimony, claiming that he had been
misinformed. But his bizarre allegation reflects his fundamental
belief that the war on terrorism and the war on drugs are inex-
tricably linked, and that the coca farmers who are forced to make
payments to the FARC are legitimate military targets, and their
neighbors' legal crops are acceptable collateral damage. Rural
Colombians pick up clearly on the message coming from the
U.S. in June, 2003, a community organizer in Cauca told me:
"Often we are mislabeled as drug traffickers or terrorists.
Nowadays with Bush, we are all terrorists. It is not just those
who plant bombs or fly planes into the Twin Towers. It is those
of us who cultivate our land and believe in the dignity of our
lives and of our country."

If John Kerry lets Rand Beers continue to guide his foreign
policy, a Kerry administration will be no better for rural
Colombians than a Bush administration. Democrats who believe
that Senator Kerry offers a humane alternative to Bush should
think long and hard about what Rand Beers would set loose on
the world.

Chapter 22

"Election cycle after election cycle the candidates flay their opponents for 'short-changing' the nation's armed forces. It's all smoke and mirrors."

Winslow Wheeler
Phonying up the Defense Budget

WINSLOW WHEELER
Phonying up the Defense Budget

TODAY, FEBRUARY 2, 2004, THE BUSH ADMINISTRATION rolls out its fiscal 2005 defense budget. Many of the things journalists will write about it will be confusing, if not misleading, and many of the prognostications from Capitol Hill, the Pentagon and the presidential candidates will be quite phony.

The press will start out with a literal confusion of numbers. A comparison across different newspaper articles will reveal that they cannot agree on the levels for the new budget, or even the old one. For fiscal year 2004, some will say it was set at $380 billion, others that it was $400 billion, and still others $462 billion. They will all be correct: the Defense Department spent $380 billion for peacetime operations; adding Department of Energy and other non-Pentagon defense spending brought it to $400 billion; and with Iraq and Afghanistan operations – that is, actually to use our forces – it cost a grand total of $462 billion. However, almost none of the articles will explain these differences.

The press will sow more chaos with what articles will say is "real" (i.e., inflation neutral) growth in the defense budget from 2004 to 2005. Few of those calculations across papers will agree. Last year, the *Washington Post* had it at 4.4 percent, *The Wall Street Journal* had it at 4.2 percent, Bloomberg news service had it at 3.8 percent, and a well-distributed trade journal, *Defense News*, had it at 6.5 percent. This year, *The Washington Post* has already had it at both 5.7 percent and 7.9 percent. Don't bother paying much attention.

First, we may not even know the size of the old 2004 defense budget, which could see another supplemental; and we certainly don't know the true size of the new 2005 budget. Wary of revealing the cost of the fighting, occupation and reconstruction in Iraq and Afghanistan (a number sure to be in the tens of billions), the administration will delay and obfuscate the ultimate costs until after the elections. Nor do we know what actual inflation rates will be for 2005, or for that matter 2004. So we can't calculate an inflation adjustment, either.

Moreover, even accurately calculated "real growth" in defense spending is a bogus concept. If we're not replacing ships and aircraft at the rate we are retiring them, which is DoD's plan, will a defense budget that increases by four, five or six percent in "real" dollars but which shrinks the size of the force mean "real growth" or "real shrinkage?"

"Real growth" gets even more misleading on an issue like military readiness for combat. Some will recall George W. Bush trashing Bill Clinton at the 2000 Republican Convention for having two Army divisions that were "not ready for duty, sir", because they had not recovered from their deployments to the Balkans. Back then, the prognosticators decided Bush was wrong because the Army conveniently rated those two divisions as "ready". But no one visited even one of the two units, as I did in September 2000, to find enormous readiness problems that Clinton's Pentagon overlooked. Today, Bush has several Army divisions and Marine units that will surely meet his own criteria for "not ready for duty, sir". One wonders if the Bush Pentagon can deal with declining readiness in a "real growth" budget any better than Clinton did.

Meanwhile, gaggles of big spender defense budget swamis and some candidates for the presidency eager to sell current defense spending as modest will claim the $420 billion for peacetime DoD spending in 2005 comes to just 3.5 percent of the Gross Domestic Product. That, they will point out, is below the 6, 8, or 10 percent we spent during the Cold War, and even below the puny 5.6 percent we spent in 1941, the year of Pearl Harbor.

These arguments are specious in the extreme. They assume there is a meaningful relationship between the size of today's larger economy and the defense budget; that defense is entitled to some particular "share" of the nation's growing wealth no matter what the nature and size of the threat. Moreover, in years when the economy is growing and the defense budget is also rising, but at a lower rate, the GDP measure shows "decline". And, if the economy is shrinking, and if defense spending were to shrink, but less, this measure would show "growth". If Bush is lucky, the economy will grow faster in 2004 than the defense budget; this will bring the "good news" that the percent of GDP for defense is falling.

These are just some of the tired and empty arguments we will hear this week as newspapers, experts and politicians chew over the defense budget. It has been this way for years. Both sides of the political spectrum have been using measures that sound like they mean something to create a meaningless or false picture. Sadly, too many press articles will only partially explain, or not at all.

Chapter 23

"Inadvertently, the Bush administration has begun to destroy an alliance system that for the world's peace should have been abolished long ago. The Democrats are far less likely to continue that process.... As dangerous as he is, Bush's reelection is much more likely to produce the continued destruction of the alliance system that is so crucial to American power in the long run.... Well before Bush took office, the Clinton administration resolved never again to allow its allies to inhibit or define its strategy. Bush's policies, notwithstanding the brutal way in which they have been expressed or implemented, follow directly and logically from this crucial decision."

Gabriel Kolko
Alliances and the American Empire

GABRIEL KOLKO
Alliances and the American Empire

ALLIANCES HAVE BEEN A MAJOR CAUSE OF WARS THROUGH-out modern history, removing inhibitions that might otherwise have caused Germany, France and countless nations to reflect much more cautiously before embarking on death and destruction. The dissolution of all alliances is a crucial precondition of a world without wars.

The United States' strength, to an important extent, has rested on its ability to convince other nations that it was to their vital interests to see America prevail in its global role. With the loss of that ability there will be a fundamental change in the international system, a change whose implications and conse-quences may ultimately be as far-reaching as the dissolution of the Soviet bloc. The scope of America's world role is now far more dangerous and ambitious than when Communism existed, but it was fear of the USSR that alone gave NATO its raison d'être and provided Washington with the justification for its global pretensions. Enemies have disappeared and new ones – many once former allies and congenial states – have taken their places. The United States, to a degree to which it is itself uncer-tain of, needs alliances. But even friendly nations are less likely than ever to be bound into complaisant "coalitions of the willing".

Nothing in President Bush's extraordinarily vague doctrine, promulgated on September 19, 2002, of fighting "preemptive" wars, unilaterally if necessary, was a fundamentally new depar-ture. Since the 1890s, regardless of whether the Republicans or Democrats were in office, the U.S. has intervened in countless ways – sending in the Marines, installing and bolstering friendly tyrants – in the western hemisphere to determine the political destinies of innumerable southern nations. The Democratic administration that established the United Nations explicitly regarded the hemisphere as the U.S. sphere of influence, and at the same time created the IMF and World Bank to police the world economy.

Indeed, it was the Democratic Party that created most of the pillars of postwar American foreign policy, from the Truman Doctrine in 1947 and NATO through the institutionalization of the arms race and the core illusion that weapons and firepower are a solution to many of the world's political problems. So the Democrats share, in the name of a truly "bipartisan" consensus, equal responsibility for both the character and dilemmas of America's foreign strategy today. President Jimmy Carter initiated the Afghanistan adventure in July 1979, hoping to bog down the Soviets there as the Americans had been in Vietnam. And it was Carter who first encouraged Saddam Hussein to confront Iranian fundamentalism, a policy President Reagan continued.

In his 2003 book *The Roaring Nineties* Joseph E. Stiglitz, chairman of the President's Council of Economic Advisers from 1993 to 1997, argues that the Clinton administration intensified the "hegemonic legacy" in the world economy, and Bush is just following along. The 1990s, Stiglitz writes, was "a decade of unparalleled American influence over the global economy" that Democratic financiers and fiscal conservatives in key posts defined, "in which one economic crisis seemed to follow another." The U.S. created trade barriers and gave large subsidies to its own agribusinesses but countries in financial straits were advised and often compelled to cut spending and "adopt policies that were markedly different from those that we ourselves had adopted." The scale of domestic and global peculation by the Clinton and Bush administrations can be debated but they were enormous in both cases. In foreign and military affairs, both the Clinton and Bush administrations have suffered from the same procurement fetish, believing that expensive weapons are superior to realistic political strategies. The same illusions produced the Vietnam War – and disaster. Elegant strategies promising technological routes to victory have been with us since the late 1940s, but they are essentially public relations exercises intended to encourage more orders for arms manufacturers, justifications for bigger budgets for the rival military services. During the Clinton years the Pentagon continued to concoct grandiose strategies, demanding – and getting – new weapons to implement them. There are many ways to measure defense expenditures over time but – minor annual fluctuations notwithstanding – the consensus between the two parties on the Pentagon's budgets has flourished since 1945. In January 2000 Clinton added $115 billion to the Pentagon's five-year plan, far more than the Republicans were calling for. When Clinton left office the Pentagon had over a half trillion dollars in the major weapons procurement pipeline, not counting the ballistic missile defense systems, a pure boondoggle that cost over $71 billion by 1999. The dilemma, as both CIA and senior Clinton officials correctly warned, was that terrorists were more likely to strike the American homeland than some nation against which the military could retaliate. This fundamental disparity between hardware and reality has always existed and September 11, 2001 showed how vulnerable and weak the U.S. has become, a theme readers can explore in my book, *Another Century of War?*

The war in Yugoslavia in the spring of 1999 brought to a head the future of NATO and the alliance, and especially Washington's deepening anxiety regarding Germany's possible independent role in Europe. Well before Bush took office, the Clinton administration resolved never again to allow its allies to inhibit or define its strategy. Bush's policies, notwithstanding the brutal way in which they have been expressed or implemented, follow directly and logically from this crucial decision.

But the world today is increasingly dangerous for the U.S. and Communism's demise has called into fundamental question the core premises of the post-1945 alliance system. More nations have nuclear weapons and means of delivering them; destructive small arms are much more abundant (thanks to swelling American arms exports which grew from 32 percent of the world trade in 1987 to 43 percent in 1997); there are more local and civil wars than ever, especially in regions like Eastern Europe which had not experienced any for nearly a half-century; and there is terrorism – the poor and weak man's ultimate weapon – on a scale that has never existed. The political, economic, and cultural causes of instability and conflict are growing, and expensive weapons are irrelevant – save to the balance sheets of those who make them.

So long as the future is to a large degree – to paraphrase Defense Secretary Donald Rumsfeld – "unknowable", it is not in the national interest of America's traditional allies to perpetuate the relationships created from 1945 to 1990. Through ineptness and a vague ideology of American power that acknowledges no limits on its global ambitions, the Bush administration has lunged into unilateralist initiatives and adventurism that discount consultations with its friends, much less the United Nations. The outcome has been serious erosion of the alliance system upon which U.S. foreign policy from 1947 onwards was based. With the proliferation of destructive weaponry and growing political instability, the world is becoming increasingly dangerous – and so is membership in alliances.

If Bush is reelected then the international order may be very different in 2008 than it is today, let alone 1999. Regardless of who is the next President, there is no reason to believe that objective assessments of the costs and consequences of its actions will significantly alter America's foreign policy priorities over the next four years. If the Democrats win they will attempt, in the name of "progressive internationalism", to reconstruct the alliance system as it existed before the Yugoslav war of 1999, when the Clinton administration turned against the veto powers built into NATO's structure. There is important bipartisan support for resurrecting the Atlanticism that Bush is in the process of smashing, and it was best reflected in the Council on Foreign Relations' banal March 2004 report on the "transatlantic alliance", which Henry Kissinger helped direct and which both influential Republicans and Wall Street leaders endorsed. Traditional elites are desperate to see NATO and the Atlantic system restored to their old glory. Their vision, premised on the expansionist assumptions that have guided American foreign policy since 1945, was best articulated the same month in a book, *The Choice: Global Domination or Global Leadership*, by Zbigniew Brzezinski, who was Carter's National Security adviser. Brzezinski rejects the Bush administration's counter-productive rhetoric that so alienates former and potential future allies. But he regards American power as central to stability in every part of world and his global vision is no less ambitious than the Bush administration's. He is for the U.S. maintaining "a comprehensive technological edge over all potential rivals" and calls for the transformation of "America's prevailing power into a co-optive hegemony – one in which leadership is exercised more through shared conviction with enduring allies than by assertive domination". Precisely because it is much more salable to past and potential allies, this traditional Democratic vision is far more dangerous than that of the inept, eccentric melange now guiding American foreign policy.

But Vice President Richard Cheney, Donald Rumsfeld, and the neoconservatives and eclectic hawks in Bush's administration are oblivious to the consequences of their recommendations or to the way they shock America's overseas friends. Many of the President's key advisers possess aggressive, essentially academic geopolitical visions that assume overwhelming American military and economic power. Eccentric interpretations of Holy Scripture inspire yet others, including Bush himself. Most of these crusaders employ an amorphous nationalist and messianic rhetoric that makes it impossible to predict exactly how Bush will mediate between very diverse, often quirky influences, though thus far he has favored advocates of wanton use of American military might throughout the world. No one close to the President acknowledges the limits of its power – limits that are political and, as Korea and Vietnam proved, military too.

Kerry voted for many of Bush's key foreign and domestic measures and he is, at best, an indifferent candidate. His statements and interviews over the past months dealing with foreign affairs have mostly been both vague and incoherent, though he is explicitly and ardently pro-Israel and explicitly for regime-change in Venezuela. His policies on the Middle East are identical to Bush's and this alone will prevent the alliance with Europe from being reconstructed. On Iraq, even as violence there escalated and Kerry finally had a crucial issue with which to win the election, his position has been indistinguishable from the President's. "Until" an Iraqi armed force can replace it, Kerry wrote in the April 13 *Washington Post*, the American military has to stay in Iraq—"preferably helped by NATO"; "no matter who is elected President in November, we will persevere in that mission" to build a stable, pluralistic Iraq – which, I must add, has never existed and is unlikely to emerge in the foreseeable future. "It is a matter of national honor and trust." He has promised to leave American troops in Iraq for his entire first term if necessary, but he is vague about their subsequent departure. Not even the scandal over the treatment of Iraqi prisoners evoked Kerry's criticism despite the fact it has profoundly alienated a politically decisive segment of the American public.

His statements on domestic policy in favor of fiscal restraint and lower deficits, much less tax breaks for large corporations, are utterly lacking in voter appeal. Kerry is packaging himself as an economic conservative who is also strong on defense spending – a Clinton clone – because that is precisely how he feels. His advisers are the same investment bankers who helped Clinton get the nomination in 1992 and then raised the funds to help him get elected and then defined his economic policy. The most important of them is Robert Rubin, who became Treasury Secretary, and he and his cronies are running the Kerry campaign and will also dictate his economic agenda should he win. These are the same men whom Stiglitz attacks as advocates of the rich and powerful.

Kerry is, to his core, an ambitious patrician educated in elite schools and anything but a populist. He is neither articulate nor impressive as a candidate or as someone who is able to formulate an alternative to Bush's foreign and defense policies, which themselves still have far more in common with Clinton's than they have differences. To be critical of Bush is scarcely justification for wishful thinking about Kerry, although every presidential election produces such illusions. Although the foreign and military policy goals of the Democrats and Republicans since 1947 have been essentially consensual, both in terms of objectives and the varied means – from covert to overt warfare – of attaining them, there have been significant differences in the way they were expressed. This was far less the case with Republican presidents and presidential candidates for most of the twentieth century, and men like Taft, Hoover, Eisenhower, or Nixon were very sedate by comparison to Reagan or the present rulers in Washington. But style can be important and inadvertently, the Bush administration's falsehoods, rudeness, and peremptory demands have begun to destroy an alliance system that for the world's peace should have been abolished long ago. In this context, it is far more likely that the nations allied with the U.S. in the past will be compelled to stress their own interests and go their own ways. The Democrats are far less likely to continue that exceedingly desirable process, a process ultimately much more conducive to peace in the world. They will perpetuate the same adventurism and opportunism that began generations ago and that Bush has merely built upon, the same dependence on military means to solve political crises, the same interference with every corner of the globe as if America has a divinely ordained mission to muck around with all the world's problems. The Democrats' greater finesse in justifying these policies is therefore more dangerous because they will be made to seem more credible and keep alive alliances that only reinforce the U.S. refusal to acknowledge the limits of its power. In the longer run, Kerry's pursuit of these aggressive goals will lead eventually to a renewal of the dissolution of alliances, but in the short-run he will attempt to rebuild them – and that is to be deplored.

CRITICS OF AMERICAN FOREIGN POLICY WILL NOT RULE WASHINGTON after this election regardless of who wins. As dangerous as he is, Bush's reelection is much more likely to produce the continued destruction of the alliance system that is so crucial to American power in the long run. Facts in no way imply moral judgments if we merely identify them. One does not have to believe that "worse is better" but we have to consider candidly the foreign policy consequences of a renewal of Bush's mandate, not the least because it is likely. Given the choices, I am not voting.

Bush's policies have managed to alienate innumerable nations. Even America's firmest allies – such as Britain, Australia, and Canada – are compelled to ask themselves if issuance of blank checks to Washington is in their national interests or if it undermines the tenure of parties in power. Foreign affairs, as the terrorism in Madrid dramatically showed in March, are too explosively volatile to permit uncritical endorsement of American policies and parties in power can pay dearly, as in Spain, where the people were always overwhelmingly opposed to entering the war and the ruling party snatched defeat from the jaws of victory. More important, in terms of cost and price, are the innumerable victims among the people. The nations that have supported the Iraq war enthusiastically, particularly Britain, Italy, the Netherlands, and Australia, have made their populations especially vulnerable to terrorism. They now have the expensive responsibility of trying to protect them.

The Washington-based Pew Research Center report on public opinion released on March 16, 2004 showed that a large and rapidly increasing majority of the French, Germans, and even British want an independent European foreign policy, reaching 75 percent in France in March 2004 compared to 60 percent two years earlier. The U.S. "favorability rating" plunged to 38 percent in France and Germany. But even in Britain it fell from 75 to 58 percent and the proportion of Britain's population who supported the decision to go to war in Iraq dropped from 61 percent in May 2003 to 43 percent in March 2004. Blair's domestic credibility, after the Labour party placed third in the June 10 local and European elections, is at its nadir. Right after the political debacle in Spain the president of Poland, where a growing majority of the people has always been opposed to sending troops to Iraq or keeping them there, complained that Washington "misled" him on Iraq's weapons of mass destruction and hinted that Poland might withdraw its 2,400 troops from Iraq earlier than previously scheduled. In Italy, by May, 2004, 71 percent of the people favored withdrawing the 2,700 Italian troops in Iraq no later than June 30, and leaders of the main opposition have already declared they will withdraw them if they win the spring 2006 elections – a promise they and other antiwar parties in Britain and Spain used in the mid-June European Parliament elections to increase significantly their power. The issue now is whether nations like Poland, Italy, or the Netherlands can afford to isolate themselves from the major European powers and their own public opinion to remain a part of the increasingly quixotic and unilateralist American-led "coalition of the willing". The political liabilities of remaining close to Washington are obvious, the advantages non-existent.

What has happened in Spain is probably a harbinger of the future, further isolating the American government in its adventures. The Bush administration sought to unite nations behind the Iraq War with a gargantuan lie – that Hussein had "weapons of mass destruction" – and failed spectacularly. Meanwhile, terrorism is more robust than ever and its arguments have far more credibility in the Muslim world. The Iraq War energized al-Qaeda and has tied down America, dividing its alliances as never before. Conflict in Iraq may escalate, as it has since March, creating a protracted armed conflict with Shiites and Sunnis that could last many months, even years. Will the nations that have sent troops there keep them there indefinitely, as Washington is increasingly likely to ask them to do? Can the political leaders afford concession to insatiable American demands?

Elsewhere, Washington opposes the major European nations on Iran, in part because the neoconservatives and realists within its own ranks are deeply divided, and the same is true of its relations with Japan, South Korea, and China on how to deal with North Korea. America's effort to assert its moral and ideological superiority, crucial elements in its postwar hegemony, is failing – badly.

America's justification for its attack on Iraq compelled France and Germany to become far more independent on foreign policy, far earlier, than they had intended or were prepared to do. In a way that was inconceivable two years ago NATO's future role is now being questioned. Europe's future defense arrangements are today an open question but there will be some sort of European military force independent of NATO and American control. Germany and France strongly oppose the Bush doctrine of preemption. Tony Blair, however much he intends to continue acting as a proxy for the U.S. on military questions, must return Britain to the European project, and his willingness since late 2003 to emphasize his nation's role in Europe reflects political necessities. To do otherwise is to alienate his increasingly powerful neighbors and risk losing elections.

Even more dangerous, the Bush administration has managed to turn what was in the mid-1990s a blossoming cordial friendship with the former Soviet Union into an increasingly tense relationship. Despite a 1997 non-binding American pledge not to station substantial numbers of combat troops in the territories of new members, NATO in March, 2003, incorporated seven East European nations and is now on Russia's very borders. Washington is in the process of establishing an undetermined but significant number of bases in the Caucasus and Central Asia. Russia has stated repeatedly that U.S. encirclement requires that it remain a military superpower and modernize its delivery systems so that it will be more than a match for the increasingly expensive and ambitious missile defense system and space weapons the Pentagon is now building. It has 5,286 nuclear warheads and 2,922 intercontinental missiles to deliver them. We now see a dangerous and costly renewal of the arms race.

Because it regards America's ambitions in the former Soviet bloc as provocation, Russia threatened in February, 2004, to pull out of the crucial Conventional Forces in Europe treaty, which has yet to come into force. "I would like to remind the representatives of [NATO]", Defense Minister Sergei Ivanov told a security conference in Munich in February, 2004, "that with its expansion they are beginning to operate in the zone of vitally important interests of our country...." By dint of its increasingly unilateral rampages, without U.N. authority, where Russia's veto power on the Security Council is, in Ivanov's wistful words, one of the "major factors for ensuring global stability", the U.S. has made international relations "very dangerous." (See Wade Boese, "Russia, NATO at Loggerheads Over Military Bases," *Arms Control Today*, March 2004; *Los Angeles Times*, March 26, 2004.) The question Washington's allies will ask themselves is whether their traditional alliances have far more risks than benefits – and if they are now necessary.

In the case of China, Bush's key advisers publicly assigned the highest priority to confronting its burgeoning military and geopolitical power the moment they came to office. But China's military budget is growing rapidly – 12 per cent this coming year – and the European Union wants to lift its 15-year old arms embargo and get a share of the enticingly large market. The Bush administration, of course, is strongly resisting any relaxation of the export ban. Establishing bases on China's western borders is the logic of its ambitions.

By installing bases in small or weak Eastern European and Central Asian nations the United States is not so much engaged in "power projection" against an amorphously defined terrorism as again confronting Russia and China in an open-ended context. Such confrontations may have profoundly serious and protracted consequences neither America's allies nor its own people have any inclination to support. Even some Pentagon analysts (see for example, Dr. Stephen J. Blank's "Toward a New U.S. Strategy in Asia," U.S. Army Strategic Studies Institute, February 24, 2004) have warned against this strategy because any American attempt to save failed states in the Caucasus or Central Asia, implicit in its new obligations, will risk exhausting what are ultimately its finite military resources. The political crisis now wracking Uzbekistan makes this fear very real.

There is no way to predict what emergencies will arise or what these commitments entail, either for the U. S. or its allies, not the least because – as Iraq proved in 2003 and Vietnam long before it – America's intelligence on the capabilities and intentions of possible enemies against which it blares its readiness to "preempt" is so utterly faulty. Without accurate information a state can believe and do anything, and this is the predicament the Bush administration's allies are in. It is simply not to their national interest, much less to the political interests of those now in power or the security of their people, to pursue foreign policies based on a blind, uncritical acceptance of fictions or flamboyant adventurism launched on false premises and information. Such acceptance is far too open-ended, both in terms of potential time and in the political costs involved. If Bush is reelected, America's allies and friends will have to confront such stark choices, a process that will redefine and probably shatter existing alliances. Many nations, including the larger, powerful ones, will embark on independent, realistic foreign policies, and the dramatic events in Spain have reinforced this likelihood.

But the United States will be more prudent, and the world will be far safer, only if it is constrained by a lack of allies and isolated. And that is happening.

Contributors

BRUCE ANDERSON is editor of the *Anderson Valley Advertiser*, America's greatest newspaper. In the summer in 2004 he moved his command post from Boonville, Northern California to Eugene, Oregon.

BRANDY BAKER lives in Baltimore, Maryland.

ROBIN BLACKBURN is author of *Banking on Death Or, Investing in Life: The History and Future of Pensions.* He's former editor of New Left Review, and author of the renowned two-volume history of colonial slavery.

ANDREW COCKBURN's most recent book, with Patrick Cockburn, is *Saddam: An American Obsession* (Verso). He lives in Washington DC.

MICHAEL DONNELLY is a grassroots forest activist and writer living in Salem, Oregon. He was a plaintiff is the first successful Old Growth lawsuit in 1986. He was active in the successful 20-year campaign to protect the magnificent forests of Oregon's Opal Creek.

SEAN DONAHUE directs the Corporations and Militarism Project of the Massachusetts Anti-Corporate Clearinghouse. He has traveled to Colombia three times on human rights delegations sponsored by Witness for Peace and the Colombia Support Network.

JOSH FRANK, a native of Montana, is a writer living in New York City. He is the author of *Left Out! : How Liberals Did Bush's Work for Him.*

KEVIN GRAY is a civil rights organizer in South Carolina and a contributing editor to *Black News* in SC. He was state coordinator of the Jackson campaign in SC in 1988.

GABRIEL KOLKO is Distinguished Research Professor Emeritus at York University in Toronto, and the leading historian of modern warfare. He is the author of the classic *Century of War: Politics, Conflicts and Society Since 1914* and *Another Century of War?*, published after the bombing of Afghanistan.

GREG MOSES is the editor of the *Texas Civil Rights Review*.

STEVE PERRY is the editor of *City Pages*, the Minneapolis weekly.

VIJAY PRASHAD teaches at Trinity College, CT. His most recent book is *Keeping Up With the Dow Joneses: Debt, Prison, Workfare* (South End Press, 2003).

JEFF TAYLOR has a PhD in political science from the University of Missouri and has been active in the Green Party since 1987. He's a member of the Olmsted County (MN) Green Party.

WINSLOW WHEELER is a Visiting Senior Fellow at the Center for Defense Information. After working for US Senators from both parties and for the US General Accounting Office for 31 years, he recently completed a book about Congress and defense policy, *The Wastrels of Defense.*

JOANN WYPIJEWSKI is a writer in New York City. Among other books she is the editor of *The Thirty Years' Wars, the collected works of Andrew Kopkind* (Verso). She was a volunteer for the Jackson campaign in the 1988 New York primary. A version of this story originally appeared in The Nation.

ALEXANDER COCKBURN and JEFFREY ST. CLAIR coedit *CounterPunch*, both the newsletter and the well-known site, www.counterpunch.org. They live, respectively, in Petrolia, Northern California and in Oregon City, Oregon.

Index

Abortion 63-72, 142, 160-1, 173
Abu-Jamal, Mumia 110
Abzug, Bella 46
ACORN 86
Adams, John 207-8, 210
Adultery 141
Affirmative action 48, 71, 89, 230-1
AFGE 86
Afghanistan war 14, 70, 162, 166-7, 254-5, 259-60, 266
AFL-CIO 10, 13
African National Congress (ANC) 80
AFSCME 86, 241
After Stonewall (Scagliotti) 6
Aid to Families with Dependent Children (AFDC) 49, 246
AIDS 90
Albright, Madeleine 63, 81
Al-Qaeda 274
Altman, Roger 27
Alyeska, Inc 200-1
American Civil Liberties Union (ACLU) 56, 57-8
American Capital Management 171-2
American Gas Association 196
American Israel Public Affairs Committee (AIPAC) 131
Amoco 158
Anderson, John 7
Andrew, Joe 176
Andrews Air Force Base (MD) 176
Angelou, Maya 96
Angola 12

Another Century of War? (Kolko) 267
Anslinger, Harry 217-8
Anti-Drug Abuse Act (1984) 221
Apartheid 80, 90
Arab-American Anti-Discrimination Committee (ADC) 81
Arabica coffee 3
Arch Coal Co 196
Arco 174, 201-2
Arctic National Wildlife Refuge (ANWR) 133, 195, 203
Arkansas Black Hall of Fame 95-6
Armstrong, Louis 217
Army Strategic Studies Institute 276
Arnett, Thomas 220-1
Ashcroft, John 63, 106
Ashland Oil Co 200
Atwater, Lee 184, 185-80
Babbitt, Bruce 199-201
Baer, Kenneth 88
Baker, Russell 124
Bane, Mary Jo 53
Bank of Credit and Commerce International (BCCI) 13
Barbour, Haley 197-8
Barral, Fernando 123-4
Baucus, Max 115-9
Baum, Dan 220
Bayh, Evan 55
Bestiality 142
Beder, Sharon 210
Beers, Rand 251
Bentham, Jeremy 40
Bentsen, Lloyd 83
Ben-Veniste, Richard 173
Berry, Mary Frances 80
Bias, Len 220
Biden, Joseph 219
Birth control 64-5
Black Entertainment Television 96

Black Issues for Higher Education (Garmon) 229
Black Radical Congress 244
Black, Hugo 4
Blackmun, Harry 70
Blair, Tony 273-4
Blank, Stephen 276
Blum, Richard 111
Boeing 174
Boese, Wade 275
Boggs, Hale 218
Boggs, Tommy 200-1
Bonaparte, Napoleon 186-7, 190
Bonds, Barry 131
Borger, Julian 22
Bositis, David 232-3
Bosnia (intervention in) 157
Boston Celtics 220
Bosworth, Dale 136
Boufis, Christina 230
Boxer, Barbara 143
Bracewell & Paterson, LLC 150
Braden, Anne 83-4, 85-6
Bradford, William 227
Bradley, Bill 67
Brennan, William 4
Brown & Foreman, Inc. 117
Brown v. the Board of Education (1954) 90, 160, 228
Brown, James 100
Brown, Ron 202
Brown, Willie 107
Bryan, William Jennings 187-8
Bryson, John 210-1
Brzezinski, Zbigniew 269
Bureau of Narcotics and Dangerous Drugs (BNDD) 217-8
Bureau of Labor Statistics (US) 24, 242

281

AK Press

ORDERING INFORMATION

AK Press
674-A 23rd Street
Oakland, CA 94612-1163
USA
(510) 208-1700
www.akpress.org
akpress@akpress.org

AK Press
PO Box 12766
Edinburgh, EH8 9YE
Scotland
(0131) 555-5165
www.akuk.com
ak@akedin.demon.uk

The addresses above would be delighted to provide you with the latest complete AK catalog, featuring several thousand books, pamphlets, zines, audio products, video products, and stylish apparel published & distributed by AK Press. Alternatively, check out our websites for the complete catalog, latest news and updates, events, and secure ordering.

Also Available from AK Press

The first audio collection from Alexander Cockburn on compact disc.

Beating the Devil

Alexander Cockburn, ISBN: 1 902593 49 9 ● CD ● $14.98

In this collection of recent talks, maverick commentator Alexander Cockburn defiles subjects ranging from Colombia to the American presidency to the Missile Defense System. Whether he's skewering the fallacies of the war on drugs or illuminating the dark crevices of secret government, his erudite and extemporaneous style warms the hearts of even the stodgiest cynics of the left.

Next from CounterPunch/AK Press

COMING FALL/WINTER, 2004

The CounterPunch Book of Monsters:
The Empire's Willing Executioners

Edited by Alexander Cockburn and Jeffrey St. Clair

The gang's all here! The Dulles Brothers, Edward Teller, The CIA's Top Poisoner, Albert Wohlstetter, the Neo-Cons Favorite Philosopher, Kissinger and his Mentor, Jeane Kirkpatrick and scores more! Who dreamed up the Tuskegee Experiment? Who Devised the Bravo H-Test? Order the CounterPunch Book of Monsters and explore the heart of darkness.

Also Available from CounterPunch and AK Press,
(call 1-800-840-3683 or order online at www.akpress.org)

Whiteout: the CIA, Drugs and the Press

by Alexander Cockburn and Jeffrey St. Clair, VERSO.

The involvement of the CIA with drug traffickers is a story that has slouched into the limelight every decade or so since the creation of the Agency. In Whiteout, here at last is the full saga.

Been Brown So Long It Looked Like Green to Me: the Politics of Nature

by Jeffrey St. Clair, COMMON COURAGE PRESS.

Covering everything from toxics to electric power plays, St. Clair draws a savage profile of how money and power determine the state of our environment, gives a vivid account of where the environment stands today and what to do about it.

The Golden Age Is In Us

by Alexander Cockburn, VERSO.

Cockburn's classic diary of the late 80s and early 90s. *"A Patchwork Paradise Lost", Times Literary Supplement. "A literary gem", Village Voice.*

Imperial Crusades: Iraq, Afghanistan and Yugoslavia

by Alexander Cockburn and Jeffrey St. Clair, VERSO

A chronicle of the lies that are now returning each and every day to haunt the deceivers in Washington and London, the secret agendas and the underreported carnage of these wars. We were right and they were wrong, and this book proves the case. Never leave home without it.

Why We Publish CounterPunch
By Alexander Cockburn and Jeffrey St. Clair

Ten years ago we felt unhappy about the state of radical journalism. It didn't have much edge. It didn't have many facts. It was politically timid. It was dull. CounterPunch was founded. We wanted it to be the best muckraking newsletter in the country. We wanted it to take aim at the consensus of received wisdom about what can and cannot be reported. We wanted to give our readers a political roadmap they could trust.

A decade later we stand firm on these same beliefs and hopes. We think we've restored honor to muckraking journalism in the tradition of our favorite radical pamphleteers: Edward Abbey, Peter Maurin and Ammon Hennacy, Appeal to Reason, Jacques René Hébert, Tom Paine and John Lilburne.

Every two weeks CounterPunch gives you jaw-dropping exposés on: Congress and lobbyists; the environment; labor; the National Security State.

"CounterPunch kicks through the floorboards of lies and gets to the foundation of what is really going on in this country", says Michael Ratner, attorney at the Center for Constitutional Rights. "At our house, we fight over who gets to read CounterPunch first. Each issue is like spring after a cold, dark winter."

YOU CANNOT MISS ANOTHER ISSUE

Name _____

Address _____

City _____ State _____ Zip _____

Email _____ Phone _____

Credit Card # _____

Exp. Date _____ Signature _____

Visit our website for more information: **www.counterpunch.org**

☐ 1 yr. **$40**   ☐ 1 yr. email **$35**   ☐ 1 yr. both **$45**
☐ 2 yr. **$70**   ☐ 2 yr. email **$60**   ☐ 2 yr. both **$80**
☐ 1 yr. low income **$30**   ☐ 2 yr. low income **$65**
☐ Supporter **$100**   ☐ Donation Only

Send Check/Money Order to: **CounterPunch, P.O. Box 228, Petrolia, CA 95558**
Canada add $12.50 per year postage. Others outside US add $17.50 per year.

The Politics of Anti-Semitism

Edited by Alexander Cockburn and Jeffrey St. Clair

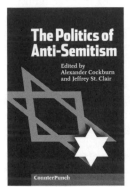

What constitutes genuine anti-Semitism – Jew-hatred – as opposed to disingenuous, specious charges of "anti-Semitism" hurled at realistic, rational appraisals of the state of Israel's political, military and social conduct?

There's no more explosive topic in American public life today than the issue of Israel, its treatment of Palestinians and its influence on American politics.

Yet the topic is one that is so hedged with anxiety, fury and fear, that honest discussion is often impossible.

The Politics of Anti-Semitism lifts this embargo.

Powerful Essays By

Michael Neumann	Scott Handleman
Alexander Cockburn	Lenni Brenner
Uri Avnery	Linda Belanger
Bruce Jackson	Robert Fisk
Kurt Nimmo	Will Youmans
M. Shahid Alam	Norman Finkelstein
Jeffrey St. Clair	Jeffrey Blankfort
George Sunderland	Kathleen and Bill Christison
Yigal Bronner	Edward Said

Reviews

"Michael Neumann's essay, "What Is Anti-Semitism," by and of itself is worth forking over the $12.95 to get a copy of The Politics of Anti-Semitism. ...There is much more in The Politics of Anti-Semitism that deserves attention. ... But, of particular note are the essay of Yigal Bronner, a member of Ta'ayush, the Arab-Jewish Partnership, and professor at Tel Aviv University, and one of the last essays of Edward Said, before he lost his life to cancer. Both of them offer a sane and humane vision in which Israelis and Palestinians are able to live together, side by side, with all their diversity and commonality, in peace. They conclude the collection fittingly, with hope for the future."

Gilles d'Aymery: www.swans.com

"This is a superlative discussion, with important lessons for all. Many of the essays in this book have appeared on the CounterPunch website – an important online magazine which is edited by the editors of this book. Cockburn, St. Clair and the other authors must be commended for addressing this important topic with this collection of excellent essays. Unfortunately, criticism of Israel is still a taboo topic, and the first ones to raise questions will probably attract a significant amount of abuse. One must remember this when appreciating the courage of those who have produced this important book."

Paul de Rooij: Washington Report on Middle East Affairs